Muffled Voices

Muffled Voices

Declan Chukwuma Umege

authorHOUSE®

AuthorHouse™
1663 Liberty Drive
Bloomington, IN 47403
www.authorhouse.com
Phone: 1-800-839-8640

Published by AuthorHouse   02/12/2013

ISBN: 978-1-4817-1075-6 (sc)
ISBN: 978-1-4817-1074-9 (hc)
ISBN: 978-1-4817-1073-2 (e)

Library of Congress Control Number: 2013901431

Chapter One

He had been standing there for more than thirty minutes now. He could have been standing for much longer because he did not care whether time passed. The only thing that bothered him now was the monstrous sight before him. The surface of the creek—the entire surface of the creek—was covered with a thick layer of glistering brown crude.

A sickening smell of crude oil hung about the entire place, a smell that offended his olfactory sense. His father's fishing nets lay in a tattered heap beside him. As his gaze fell on the heap, a tear rose from his eye and ran down his cheek. He looked in the direction of the fish pond, which now looked like a graveyard. The once robust and beautiful species of fish were floating on the surface with no iota of life in them.

"Tamuna!" his father called.

"Yes, father," he answered.

"Come, let's go home."

Tamuna gathered the battered fishing nets and put them in the big basket, the one meant for carrying home fish. His father took one last glance at his devastated fish pond, shook his head, and set out for the return journey home. They walked slowly in silence.

The surrounding block of mangrove forest look vacant, deathly, and scotched. Tamuna stumbled on a protruding root of a dying tree of mangrove origin (another victim of many years of oil pollution) and almost lost his balance.

"Tamuna!" his father called.

"Yes, father," he answered.

"Be careful or you'll injure yourself."

"Yes, father," Tamuna answered.

When they got home, Tamuna set out for the stream, which was about four kilometers away. The stream water is itchy on the skin, even after a bath, due to the oil pollution and gases from the oil flares. For the average inhabitant of Tembeli Kingdom, there was no choice. Oilgate, the major multinational oil company in them, had donated a pipe-borne water scheme to Tembeli, but it had broken down long ago. No genuine effort had been made to resuscitate it.

Tamuna hurriedly made two trips to the stream, took his bath, and prepared for school. Other domestic chores were left for the younger ones.

After breakfast, Tamuna got into his school uniform and left for school. The bush path, the shortest route to school, seemed lonelier than ever. Tamuna, however, was not bothered that he would have to trek to school without company. Instead, he looked forward to his academic activities at school.

Tamuna attended Tembeli International School, a school originally built for the wards of the expatriate community in Tembeli Kingdom. Also in attendance were the wards of privileged citizens of Tembeli. By virtue of their association with the government or the white community or their financial *locus standi*, they could afford to foot the bills for the school.

Tamuna is a peasant boy—no more or less than all other peasant boys born in his generation in the oil-rich Kingdom of Tembeli. When he was a kid, a mere toddler, an event took place in his town. He was nearly fourteen but could still remember vividly the event that marked a turning point in his life.

His father, Ledum, was a farmer. Ledum cultivated a few crops to meet the needs of his immediate family, but his area of specialization was fish farming. As the saying goes in Tembeli, he carved a niche for himself in fish farming. He loved fishing so much that, sometimes, when he went to bed, he would murmur new strategies that he intended to employ in his fishing practice. He claimed he received inspiration from dreams in terms of how and where to go fishing.

Ledum owned many fishing boats and nets. Fishermen from far and near came to him to borrow his boats and fishing nets. In return, such fishermen paid with a portion of their catches. It has always been said that if one wants to be more successful than one's peers, one should do what others have not done. Such was the case with Ledum: he was the first fish farmer in Tembeli (and beyond) to own a fish pond. His popularity grew throughout Tembeli Kingdom and other areas. A mere mention of his name could fetch one a great favor.

Besides being a wealthy man, Ledum was a man noted for his love for truth. This singular quality endeared him to all men, women, and children. He was fearless; he would always speak the truth—to the amazement and disappointment of some of his kinsmen. Ledum became a man who could be trusted, one who could be given the mandate to steer others to clear waters without any sign of fear. Ledum became the custodian of the people's dreams, hopes, and aspirations. He was elected to one office after another. He became a vital human force in Tembeli Kingdom, and he could easily get people to support whatever noble view he had.

Oilgate saw him as a threat to their continued exploitation of the natural oil wealth in the bosom of Tembeli Kingdom. They monitored him very closely.

A time came when Oilgate awarded a contract to one of its indigenous contractors to lay oil pipelines through Tembeli Kingdom in order to transport crude oil from their crude oil flow stations to their terminal for export. Farm lands were destroyed, and newly planted crops were bulldozed in the process. The site was a disaster. Ben Sare, the leader of the Tembeli Liberation Movement, supported men of Ledum's caliber. He mobilized support for adequate compensation for the affected farmers. In the end, however, no compensation was distributed.

Oilgate's pipe-laying contractor was forced to stop his pipe-laying job amid protest from the host communities. Consequently, the military government of Muzanga moved in and mobilized mobile policemen. They stormed the protest ground, beating and arresting key players in the game.

Ben Sare escaped. Ledum also escaped, and so did other notable leaders of the liberation movement. The military government of Muzanga was disappointed.

Ledum was trailed and arrested in his house after several weeks of fruitless search. He was bound in handcuffs and beaten into a coma. His entire household was in tears. Tamuna wept his soul out. Ledum was later bundled into a police jeep and driven to the state capitol. He was locked up and charged for taking the law into his own hands.

The sight of his father—his beloved and cherished father—being treated like a criminal shattered Tamuna's childhood dreams. His dreams of growing up under the care of his all-powerful father were dashed.

If the police can mistreat my father the way they did, no soul in Tembeli Kingdom is safe, Tamuna thought. Some days afterward, when his father came out of the police cell (looking thin and sickly), it dawned on Tamuna that something had to be done to protect his father. Something had to be done to protect the Tembeli Kingdom. *The goose that lays the golden egg must not be allowed to die,* Tamuna thought.

His father told his immature mind how Oilgate, in a deadly romance with the military government of Muzanga, was gradually carting away the oil wealth of Tembeli Kingdom.

After nearly ten years, his father's words still echoed in Tamuna's subconscious mind.

"My son, these people want all of us dead. They have sucked our oil—our God-given oil—leaving behind cries of agony. How can you smack a child and tell him not cry?"

"See, my son. Go to the sites where they flare their gases—the palm trees there can no longer bear fruit. Tilapia caught at some of the flare sites have lost the ability to change color; they become rubbery when cooked. Some staple foods of Tembeli Kingdom can no longer germinate and grow in our soil. Why? They have debased our soil and made it sterile. The red and white varieties of cocoyam and mammy yam have become extinct. Even the local varieties of rice and oil palm have been recording lower yields over the years."

Ledum continued, "As a boy, my father used to buy me and my brothers Christmas clothes from proceeds from his catches. He made these catches not in the river, but just at the waterfronts where boys would gather leisurely to catch fish. But today, fishermen in Tembeli Kingdom spend about eight hours or more in the river (at long distances) only to return with no catch at all.

"Oil pollution has killed nearly all our fish and driven the surviving ones to the very high seas.

"The swamp of the mangrove forest, home to what used to be countless periwinkles (a traditional delicacy of Tembeli Kingdom), is equally threatened. The periwinkles are gradually becoming extinct. Pollution has gradually driven off the monkeys and antelopes, which used to inhabit the forest.

"Top of the heap of endangered animals are the inhabitants of Tembeli kingdom. Traditionally, the people depend on rain water to drink and do their domestic chores (because the creeks and most rivers are salty). Decade of gas flaring has made the rain water acidic and full of salt.

"My son, we don't bury the dead and go to remove the bodies. That is not our custom. Nevertheless, Oilgate has forcefully removed the graves of our ancestors to the oceans to get access routes to their well heads. We must fight them. Only men like Ben Sare can fight them adequately. We need more of such men in this great kingdom to win the fight.

"They have guns and bullets, but we will not fight back with guns and bullets. We need just one weapon: *education*.

"You must go to school, my son, and acquire as much learning as you can. You must read like Ben Sare so you can fight them with your pen and wisdom."

As fate would have it, Tamuna was instantly successful when he started primary school. He was the pupil everybody wanted to beat academically. He finished primary school with flying colors, and he won a scholarship, the Ben Sare Academic Award for Excellence, to attend the prestigious Tembeli International School (TIS).

At school, Tamuna was determined to excel. He read his books. He was neither going to disappoint his father nor his kingdom. He was not going to disappoint Ben Sare, *the liberator*, whose scholarship earned him a place at TIS. Tamuna longed to meet him, but he knew he had to be like him first. He must gain knowledge—plenty of knowledge—and then he could join in the struggle to save his beloved kingdom.

Chapter Two

At school, Tamuna continued to shine like a million stars. As the year passed by (and he graduated from one class to the next), his academic brilliance dazzled all who came in contact with him—students and teachers alike. His superior mental abilities were always displayed whenever the need arose. One such occasion was during his speech, on Speech Day.

Speech Day is an annual event in Tembeli International School that brings together parents, guardians, resource persons, and all the crème de la crème of society. Such events provide an excellent opportunity for students to present topics of interest with a view to mirroring the school's academic standards.

*   *   *

Today is Speech Day, and Tembeli International School is looking the part. Grass has been trimmed throughout the school's compound. The main road leading to the school has been adorned with white painted stones. When observed from a distance, they are impressive to behold. Here and there, one can see red and white patches on tree trunks. Flowers have been planted in designated areas of the school's compound.

The school's auditorium, the venue of the speech, looked magnificent. The seats shone, and the stage waited in yawning anticipation. The microphone was adorned with aluminum decorations that glittered and danced with grace as the gentle breeze from the standing fan blew from side to side.

The staff at Tembeli International School did an excellent job at making the school ready to host the august visitors. The students also worked tirelessly to keep the compound neat. Tamuna was not a part of the tidying up process, however, because he had been chosen to deliver a speech on this great occasion.

Tamuna was seated under the foot of an umbrella tree, sending his thoughts on errands in preparation for the speech.

He heard the sound of approaching footsteps. His chain of thought was immediately broken. He knew instinctively that the footsteps were headed toward him. He glanced sideways and saw Anita walking toward him, a smile of innocence written on her face. Anita's approaching form made Tamuna's brain flash back in time to his mind-blowing presentation during a history lesson. His presentation was titled *The Scramble for Africa.*

Most of Tamuna's classmates had been of the opinion that colonialism was the best thing to happen to Africa. They had based their arguments on the gains of colonialism, such as Western education. Tamuna had a different view entirely, having read wildly and widely.

Tamuna told his classmates the following: "The white man came to our beloved continent, Africa. For 500 years, the white man carted away our young men into slavery. Our entire workforce was destroyed. The youth, upon whose shoulders the future of Africa rested, were forcefully removed to Europe during the transatlantic slave trade. There, they were made to tame plantations of the white men. They were subjected to conditions below the crudeness of nature, below the lives of the lower species.

"When Europe entered the era of the industrial revolution, machines took the place of human beings in production. Slaves were no longer needed; thus, the slave trade was abolished. When they recognized that their fast-growing industries in Europe needed raw materials, they turned to Africa and used colonialism as the tool to perpetrate their selfish motives.

"For another one hundred years, Africa lived in bondage under the tutelage of colonialism. They came with their schools. The primary aim of these schools was to train Africans to help them administer their colonies (instead of training them to be self-reliant). Colonial schooling was education for subordination and exploitation. It created mental confusion and developed underdevelopment.

"They made our economy totally dependent on theirs. They used economic jargon to support their dubious intentions. They made us believe in international trade, that we should produce goods for export. We were told that our cocoa, palm produce, groundnuts, etc. should be exported to Europe because we had a comparative advantage over Europe in those crops. They dubbed them cash crops. What they failed to explain to us, however, was that local industries could be set up to use the goods rather than exporting them to the West."

Tamuna received a standing ovation from his class when he finished his presentation. It was clear that he had exhibited an impeccable mental prowess. Tamuna became the cynosure of all eyes. Everybody wanted to be identified with him.

After school that day, Anita walked up to him and said flatly, "Your presentation blew my mind away."

Tamuna was extremely pleased that such a frank remark came from Anita because she was one of the few students who exuded confidence in his class. Not only was she brilliant, but she was also one of the few privileged students who were chauffeur-driven to and from school.

All the trappings of the upper echelon didn't matter to Tamuna, though, because he was determined to prove to all that superiority came from how sound one was upstairs rather than how much one had in his or her pocket.

"I have looked for you everywhere," Anita said.

Tamuna was brought back to the present. "How are you doing, Anita?" he asked.

"I am fine. Thank you," she replied. She sat down beside him and observed him calmly.

"I broke away from the confusion of the moment to see whether I could put finishing touches on my speech," Tamuna said.

"That is all right. You know, a lot of people out there believe in your ability to add bite to the occasion."

"Bite? But I haven't got the teeth of an Alsatian—how can I add bite to the occasion?"

Anita chuckled and said, "Look, I came to tell you one thing: you must not let me down with your presentation."

Before Tamuna could respond to the statement, Anita got to her feet and walked toward the school's auditorium, the venue of the speech.

*   *   *

At precisely 10.00 am, it was clear that a sizable number of guests had arrived for Speech Day at Tembeli International

School. The school's alarm was sounded a couple of times to announce to all that the event was about to commence.

Students started to detach themselves from the groups they had formed, and they started to head in the direction of the school's auditorium.

As usual, the auditorium was beautiful. The only difference was that tables and chairs had been arranged on either side of the stage for the guests.

The auditorium was filled to capacity by students and teachers alike. Somewhere in the crowd—tucked in among the numerous heads that dotted the auditorium—sat Tamuna. The guests were nowhere in sight.

Mr. Jack, the senior history master, walked to the stage and grabbed the microphone. Mr. Jack wielded great popularity in Tembeli International School, partly due to his knowledge of global politics. When he stood to talk to an audience, his Marxist tone made one wonder whether he was a teacher or a revolutionary. Tamuna loved Mr. Jack's perspectives on issues, and he saw him as a model through whom he could shape his personality.

In turn, Mr. Jack had a secret admiration for the young man. He saw him as a revolutionary volcano waiting to erupt at any moment.

Mr. Jack made a short speech to reassure the audience that all was well. He then said he was going to introduce the master of ceremonies. There were incoherent murmurs from the audience because master of ceremonies cap fit Mr. Jack better than any other teacher in TIS. Shortly after, he introduced himself as the MC, and a rousing applause followed.

The guests were later introduced by Mr. Jack, and they seemed to be appearing from nowhere. In attendance were the representatives of the expatriate community in Tembeli Kingdom, two representatives of Oilgate International, the mayor of Tembeli Kingdom, and fifteen representatives of TIS. The principal of TIS took his place among the guests. He was a fine gentleman with many years of school administration in his kitty.

When it was time for the principal to present his welcome address to the audience, he exhibited a high degree of mental alertness and an unparalleled sense of humor. He spoke with an air of custodianship, stressing the achievements of the school during the last few years, the areas in which the school needed assistance, and the need for parents and guardians to pay unscheduled visits to the school to ascertain the school's rate of progress.

The chairman of the occasion, Honorable Isaac Birago, the mayor of Tembeli Kingdom, was next to speak. To the average Tembelite, the mayor was a stooge of the military government of Muzanga and Oilgate International. In several cases of environmental abuses and exploitation perpetrated in Tembeli Kingdom by Oilgate, the mayor appeared disinterested. It was even rumored that the election that ushered him into the mayorship position was grossly manipulated in his favor.

In Tembeli, the mayor was seen as an instrument of subjugation and exploitation. As Tamuna sat watching the mayor deliver his welcome address, bitter memories of his sinister collaborations with the government and Oilgate flooded his mind.

Tamuna's spirit, however, came alive when members of the school's choral society rendered three beautiful songs in quick succession. The presentations were superbly sonorous, and the students' faces beamed with joy.

Tamuna could not say, however, whether it was the presence of Anita in the group that made him drift into ecstasy as the music played.

After the songs, the guests and the teachers were treated to a tea break. The period saw members of the dramatic society of TIS swing into action. Their drama presentation was short, and the message was explicitly conveyed to the audience.

And then came the moment Tamuna had been waiting for: the moment in which he would deliver his speech. Tamuna had been asked to talk about the youth as leaders of the future.

Tamuna got to his feet and slowly walked to the rostrum. A round of applause seemed to follow every step he took.

He grabbed the microphone and bowed respectfully to the distinguished guests and the audience. The applause that followed was deafening.

"Distinguished ladies and gentlemen," Tamuna started. He then paused to look at the thousands of faces glued to his face.

"Right at this moment—while we are all seated here—there is a revolution going on the world over. It is neither the violent kind of revolution that has ushered in leaders of nation nor the nonviolent type that is aimed at bringing about a colossal change in the way nations are being governed. It is a revolution whose target is the youth, and its aim is total empowerment for the challenges of tomorrow.

A great applause followed, and Tamuna waited for it to die down before he continued.

"The youth form the bridge between the aging population and the infants. They are, unquestionably, the pivot on which any society stands. The youth hold the key to the survival of any race, be it black or white. Exterminate the youth, and you wipe out a generation."

Tamuna paused and looked from one end of the auditorium to another. Everybody was staring at him with rapt attention. He dipped his hand into his left hip pocket, brought out his handkerchief, and mopped his face. He continued: "It is important to empower our youth so they can stand shoulder high, like their counterparts in other parts of the world! Should basic education not be the right of every youth?

"Gentlemen and ladies, how can we all be seated here and pretend that all is well with the youth of this generation? In order for the youth to attain a leadership status (as we all expect), the youth must be allowed to grow. Unfortunately, circumstances have made the youth so stunted that growth only lives in the firmament of imagination.

"What leadership qualities do we expect the youth to develop when they are growing up in an environment where killing, maiming, and insecurity reign supreme? An environment charged with intimidation and associated frustration and hopelessness—where our youth find themselves today—has nothing to offer.

"For our vision of tomorrow to be realized, we must start today to pursue realistic plans and programs that are aimed at redirecting the colossal energies of our youths into nonviolent and useful forms."

There was a great applause from the audience as Tamuna ended his speech. Some of his admirers, especially students, got to their feet as Tamuna made his way to his seat slowly.

Chapter Three

His alarm bell went into a series of controlled vibrations. Tamuna awoke from his sleep and slammed his fist against the knob. The alarm system stopped immediately. He checked what the time was—a few minutes past five o'clock in the morning.

Everything and everybody was calm in the hostel. Only the incoherent murmurs of students approaching dreamland (and the deep snores of those already there) broke the silence of the hostel. Besides these subtle sounds, absolute quietude reigned.

Tamuna hurriedly got into his clothes, picked up his bag (previously packed the night before), and left the hostel after closing the door silently behind him. He had to avoid the major path that went across the school's compound for fear of being spotted by the school's security personnel.

From a distance, a dog barked. And that bark was followed by another and another. Tamuna stood still; he remained motionless, like a statue. After what seemed like a quarter of an hour—when silence had again descended upon the school's compound—Tamuna continued on his way.

He was heading for a familiar spot: the log from a Gmelina tree that rested beside the school's barbed wire. It would provide the best leverage for jumping across the barbed wire.

Tamuna walked across small roads and behind buildings. He could have been mistaken for a ghost in the dim light of the school's compound. He got to the spot at last, burst into a sprint, reached the fence, stepped on the log, and leapt into space. He shut his eyes in the process, and it seemed like an eternity before he landed with a crash on the other side of the fence. He remained where he was for a few minutes and watched his surroundings. When he was convinced that his crash landing had attracted no attention, he got up, straightened his clothes, picked up his bag, and disappeared into the fading darkness of dawn.

*   *   *

The mission compound, which houses the church and mission school, was packed with people. There were so many people there that Tamuna wondered whether they were all sons and daughters of Tembeli Kingdom.

Tamuna had not been fully informed of the magnitude, nature, and mode the rally would assume. All he knew was that there was going to be a peace rally, and he was expected to be in attendance. It was Mr. Jack who passed the information to Tamuna.

Earlier, when Tamuna arrived home from school, he was surprised to find that no adult was home. All had gone to the venue of the rally. He wasted no time heading to the mission compound where the epoch-making rally was taking place.

When Tamuna arrived at the venue of the rally, he beheld a mammoth crowd. Every member of the crowd seemed to be facing one particular direction. There were people in trees and atop buses. Some rode on the shoulders of others, and they all waited with patience for a chance to catch a glimpse of the man on the elevated platform. The man was talking to the crowd, and he had the aura of a politician who cared only for manifesto rhetoric.

All Tamuna could see of the man from where he stood was a broad chest. He could tell he was a powerfully built man of middle age who was clad in a native safari suit. He had a smoking pipe in his left hand.

The smoking pipe made an impression on Tamuna's mind. It was not that he had not seen that type of pipe before; rather, he had heard of the man with the smoking pipe: Ben Sare, the liberator. Tamuna was immediately engulfed with anticipatory excitement as he edged his way through the mammoth crowd.

*   *   *

Tamuna was thrilled at the way Ben Sare spoke. His speech was packed with so much revolutionary force that Tamuna longed for a closer encounter with him. He felt the man was a kindred spirit.

After the speech, Tamuna watched as people fell into groups of fifties and one hundreds. They broke away gradually from the teeming crowd and began to chant solidarity songs. There were boys, girls, men, and women—and they all fell into their respective age groups. They carried placards with different types of inscriptions, but they all contained one principal message: "Oilgate and the military government of Muzanga are conspirators in the exploitation of the God endowed wealth of Tembeli kingdom."

Some of the carriers of these placards were not literate enough to interpret the message they carried, but deep in their hearts, the message was indelibly inscribed there. With their last drop of blood, they were ready to oppose whomever stood between them and their destiny (and the destiny of their children and those yet unborn).

When Tamuna joined his group, he discovered that some of his peers in the village were already there. He gladly joined them. Although they might have wanted to exchange pleasantries with him, the scene called for serious business.

Once in a while, a young lad would dash in front of the group, dancing and chanting solidarity songs while the rest of the group join in with the chorus. Tamuna quickly blended in with the crowd because he had spent all his childhood days in the village.

Time and again, Tamuna would dash forward to lead the group. The manner in which he chanted his songs inspired militant feelings among his peers. He would change back and forth from his native songs to English, especially the ones he learnt from Mr. Jack. Occasionally, he tried to retire to the crowd to give another person the chance to play the lead role, but they would urge him to go on and on.

The protesters surged forward militantly. The scene being played out was reminiscent of the one played back in the time of the biblical exodus of the Israelites out of Egypt. As the crowd marched through the major streets in Tembeli, non-Tembelites and visitors of all ages came out to watch the epoch-making march.

The first port of call of the protesters was the local government area headquarters. When they arrived, the civil servants there had mixed feelings. Although many of them would gladly have joined the rally, they could not for fear of losing their jobs. The atmosphere was charged with excitement. Press cameras flashed here and there with reckless abandon. The security officials at the headquarters were helpless; they could not stop the protesters. On and on, the protesters surged forward like soldier ants.

The local government administrator was not in sight. Obviously, he took to the bush through the exit route. The protest was not aimed at breaching the peace; instead, the aim was to show dissatisfaction about the overall state of affairs in Tembeli Kingdom.

After what seemed like an hour of peaceful protest throughout the local government headquarters, Ben Sare appeared from within the crowd. He stood on a hastily constructed and elevated platform, and he addressed the crowd. It took him about three minutes to calm everyone down. He spoke. He reminded them why they were there, how to go about the protest, and how not to go about the protest. After all, their aim was not to cause turmoil. He then went on to talk about the injustices being perpetrated jointly by the military government of Muzanga and Oilgate International.

As he spoke, pressmen had a field day trying to bring the liberator into focus. When he had finished talking, he raised a song—a militant one—and the crowd chorused in ecstasy.

Next, the protesters marched to the mayor's residence. There, the protesters met a little resistance. The armed policemen at the gate threatened to shoot if the protesters did not retreat. Their dangerous-looking Alsatian dogs kept barking aggressively. The policemen fired teargas into the air. Some protesters ran for cover; some stood their ground, determined to storm the compound.

Some youth got beaten up by policemen. When the protesters saw it was impossible to gain access into the compound without causalities, they regrouped and stormed out into the streets.

They headed for the expatriate quarters. The quarters were guarded day and night by heavily armed security agents. Entry would definitely be very difficult because the security officials would not tolerate passersby.

The protesters were still about 3000 meters away from the expatriate quarter's entrance when, from a distance, the sound of a police siren tore through the sounds of protesting voices. The mobile policemen arrived on the scene, and the protesters ran in all directions.

There was a shootout for several hours. The mobile policemen used a combination of live bullets and rubber bullets. The youth resisted the inhuman treatment of the armed mobile policemen. Human bodies fell to the ground like sacks of grain, and yet the youth fought back with improvised weapons.

In the end, 250 persons were dead, and over 1,000 were injured.

Chapter Four

Tamuna used the free period in his school's daily academic timetable to have some quiet time in the library. He was pestered by his friends and acquaintances, though. They kept asking him unending questions. In the hostel, at the playground, in the classroom—virtually everywhere—Tamuna was besieged by streams of questions.

"Did you participate in the rally?" "Did you speak at the rally?" "How many people really died?" "Did anybody?"

The questions echoed in Tamuna's mind. Of course, he denied ever having left the school's compound during the period the rally took place. Although his absence had been noticed the day the rally took place, he smartly sneaked back to school before dusk, in time for the hostel's roll call by the house master.

When news of the rally and casualty figure hit the airwaves, the school's authority instructed all the hostel masters to carry out a roll call of all students in the boarding house. The result of the roll call was amazing: no student of TIS was missing. Still there was speculation that some of the indigenous students of Tembeli Kingdom, especially the young revolutionary dynamite, Tamuna, might be involved.

The dailies vividly captured the intense moments of the rally. The *Daily Times* had the following caption: "Midday Massacre in Tembeli Kingdom" on its front page. *The Guardian* newspaper front page caption read: "Blood Flows in Tembeli Kingdom." *The Vanguard* reported: "Black Gold Saga Hit the Nation." *The National Statesman* reported: "Crisis in Tembeli Kingdom—the Nation's Oil Wealth Threatened."

According to the story, there was bloodshed and confusion in Tembeli Kingdom. That bloodshed followed an aborted peaceful demonstration of Tembeli people at the hands of men from the mobile police force. 250 persons were killed and over 1000 were injured. The story went on to say that Tembeli Kingdom was a distinct ethnic group, numbering over 500,000 and inhabiting the coastal plain terrace north of the Niger Delta. They were described as the geese that laid the golden eggs for the nation's economy.

Oilgate International, a multinational oil company, struck oil in Tembeli Kingdom in 1959. Over one billion barrels of oil have been drilled from the area since then.

There were said to be more than one hundred oil wells that were connected to eight oil fields in Tembeli kingdom. In those oil fields, gas was flared day and night for over four decades. Oilgate International's pipelines were said to crisscross the entire surface of Tembeli Kingdom. Beyond the pipelines and oil fields, a fertilizer plant, an oil refinery, a petrochemical plant, and two sea ports were set up in Tembeli Kingdom.

When Tembelites took stock of their condition, they found that, despite their oil and gas wealth, they were extremely poor and had an alarming unemployment rate. They were powerless as an ethnic minority group in Muzanga republic (which consisted of over 200 million people). Worse, their environment was being completely devastated due to decades of reckless oil exploitation. Tembeli Kingdom was facing environmental degradation, political marginalization, economic strangulation, slavery, and possible extinction.

The story went on to say that the chiefs and leaders of Tembeli Kingdom adopted a bill that granted, among other things, the right to use a fair portion of the economic resources of their land for development and control over their environment. These demands were presented to the military government of Muzanga.

After more than two years, the people of Tembeli Kingdom—under the leadership of the Tembeli Liberation Movement (TLM)—presented Oilgate with a ninety-day notice. The mandate read as follows: "Pay back rent and royalties in addition to compensation for devastated land or leave Tembeli Kingdom.'

While staging a peaceful demonstration to reaffirm their mandate, members of the mobile police force descended on the people with bullets.

Tamuna looked from the newspaper to the window that overlooked the school's administration block. Bitter memories flooded his mind, memories of an ungodly alliance between Oilgate and the military government of Muzanga. The most bitter revelation was the fact that the government seemed to have provided Oilgate with the backing they needed to further milk Tembeli Kingdom dry.

"No!" Tamuna shouted aloud. Immediately, he came to the realization that he had allowed his emotions to overtake him. Students in the library looked in his direction. He apologized.

He tried to read further, but his thoughts were in disarray. He looked at his left wrist and ran his finger over the bruises he sustained during the rally while attempting to run for cover.

Tamuna wondered what his father's present state of health might be. His father, Ledum, had sustained a gun-shot wound on his abdomen, and he lay groaning in pain while thousands of escaping feet trampled over him. By the time he was discovered, he had lost consciousness and lay in a pool of his own blood. The doctors at the community hospital later placed him in the intensive care unit of the hospital.

As Tamuna thought about his wounded father and several others whose fates hung in the balance, tears formed in his eyes and ran down his cheeks. He fished inside his pocket for his handkerchief and dried his tears.

The mortuary had been littered with dead bodies, and Tembeli was akin to a valley of tears. Tamuna thought, *But what about Ben Sare, the leader of the liberation movement? Was he dead or injured? Had he escaped?* The answers refused to form in Tamuna's mind. One thing was certain: the death of the liberator would cast a dark shadow on the liberation struggle.

Chapter Five

Ben Sare hastily moved from the arrival wing of the Geneva International Airport to the busy hum of the street. The events of the past few days had made an indelible impression on his mind. The events made him vow to defend his people—the powerless people of Tembeli Kingdom—with all his material and intellectual resources . . . even his own life.

He had sneaked out of the country's borders disguised as a woman and flown to Geneva to solicit international support for Tembeli Kingdom. He also presented a paper on environmental and human rights violations in the Niger Delta on World Environmental Day celebration in Geneva.

Ben Sare—writer, lawyer, and environmentalist—always maintained a very simple appearance wherever he went. He was easily spotted in gatherings. He usually dressed in a native safari suit, which gave him the appearance of a traditional African prince. One distinctive feature of his appearance was his pipe. He smoked his pipe in the most admirable fashion. He was about fifty years old, and he could have passed for a boxer during his youthful days due to his broad chest and powerful, muscular build.

As he stood by the thoroughfare and waited for a taxi, some sweat started to form on his forehead. He mopped it with his handkerchief as he hopped in a cab.

"Take me to Hotel de Eldorado," he said.

"Sure, sir," replied the cab driver as he kicked the car's engine into life and zoomed off.

* * *

The atmosphere in the room was tense. One's imagination could easily be beaten by the fact that there were about four hefty men in the room, yet the sound of a pin dropping to the floor could be heard easily. There were five seats arranged in a semi-circle around the small conference table. One seat, however, was vacant.

Alan Fisher, the technical director at Oilgate International sat at one end of the table. He was in his early fifties, and he exuded an aristocratic aura. He had been at the helm of Oilgate's technical affairs for the past decade.

Joseph Carpenter, a bespectacled fifty-two-year-old man from the Netherlands sat next to Mr. Fisher. Carpenter was the financial director at Oilgate International. At the other end of the conference table sat Tunde Idowu and Obi Maduekwe, the deputy managing director and head of public and government affairs, respectively.

The vacant seat at the center of the arc was meant for the managing director of Oilgate International, Bill Smith. The meeting was expected to commence when Mr. Smith arrived.

There was silence in the room—each man seemed to prefer studying documents to speaking.

After what seemed like a quarter of an hour, the door leading into the conference arena was thrown widely open, and Bill Smith bulldozed his way into the room. He headed straight for the vacant seat at the center of the arc and sat down.

There was no exchange of greetings, no exchange of pleasantries, no shaking of hands. Nothing. The room became silent again.

Next, Bill Smith got to his feet. He surveyed the others briefly and adjusted his spectacle on the bridge of his nose. Bill was a sixty years old. He had been the Managing Director of Oilgate International for one complete term, and he was in the middle of his second.

"Gentlemen," he started, "our mission this morning should be finding an immediate solution to the crisis that is about to rock our company. We have sunk billions of dollars into exploration, drilling, and production of the crude oil reserve in Tembeli, and we must not fold our hands and watch an ego-seeking environmentalist send all our investments down the drains." He paused and surveyed the others once again before speaking: "That brat and his movement! If he thinks he can put us out of business, he is mistaken. The big question is, what do we do to stop this menace?"

Bill Smith sat down and Alan Fisher got to his feet to speak. "In my opinion, Ben Sare and his movement are making empty threats—that is what I call it. How could he think that, after our multibillion—dollar investment, we would simply leave due to some ninety-day nonsense? He must be a joker! What he fails to understand is that, if we stop business, his country's economy crumbles. After all, oil accounts for over ninety percent of his country's revenue. The key to this economy rests in our hands.

"I think we need to consult relevant government agencies extensively before this crazy guy pulls the rug out from under our feet. The government should be made to understand that it is its duty to provide us with an environment that enables us to do our legitimate business.

"In the past, we used to build roads and hospitals. The government came with its Fund for the Development of Oil Producing Areas (FUNDOPA), and it mandated that we contribute. Do the funds not take care of the communities? The government cannot fold its hands and watch these traitors put our investment into jeopardy. It is not our business what the government does with the funds, but one thing is clear: we must remain in business."

No sooner had Alan Fisher sat down than Obi Maduekwe got to his feet. As the man at the helm of government and public affairs, he was in a better position to proffer an adequate solution to the present logjam.

"Gentlemen," he started, "it is clear that the culprit in this deadly game is the military government of Muzanga. We pay our dues to the government, we pay into FUNDOPA. The government appoints the chiefs and administrators for these communities (who are supposed to receive the monies to develop their communities). We even go the extra mile by providing some basic social amenities. But now we are being accused of environmental violations and crimes.

"It is true that the compensation we offer is nothing compared to what is obtainable in Europe and America, but at least we give them what they ask for. So where have we erred? We must speak with the military government of Muzanga immediately and advance our grievances to them."

The other men also spoke, and the meeting progressed. After what seemed like four hours of heated debate, they took a tea break, which signaled the end of the first stormy meeting.

*   *   *

Tamuna flipped through the pages of the dailies, looking for articles of interest. The morning lectures had been boring for him because his mind was focused on the crisis in the land. He had to excuse himself in the middle of a history lesson and went straight to the school's library.

Unable to find an article of interest, Tamuna turned to the sports column for soccer news. He read the column without interest. His mind drifted back to the rally. He felt really bitter. He rested his head on the table and dozed off.

After what seemed like an hour, a tap on his shoulder brought him back from dreamland. He awoke and beheld Anita.

"Anything the matter?" Anita asked, sitting down beside him.

"No, I am all right," Tamuna lied.

"The fact is, I have a slight headache. That is all."

"How about going to the school's clinic?"

"I won't bother—I'll be okay."

"Well, if you say so," Anita said, getting to her feet.

When Anita left, Tamuna realized that he should have bared his mind to her. Doing so would have eased the emotional load because she was someone who really cared.

Chapter Six

His Excellency, the head of state (HOS) and commander-in-chief of Muzanga Republic, General Shehu Mohammed, paced around his exquisitely furnished sitting room. He waited in anticipation for his aide-de-camp (ADC). He had detailed his ADC to summon members of the national ruling council for an emergency meeting to discuss the state of affairs in the nation.

He fished inside his pocked and pulled out a pack of cigarettes. He lit one up in his trembling hands, inhaled the smoke very deeply, shook his head, and smiled mischievously as he said, "That man. I will definitely nail him. He doesn't know who he is messing around with."

The HOS was indeed greatly troubled by the latest developments in his country. If events were brought to a head and the nation's oil was boycotted in the international oil market, it would be an absolute disaster. His dream of a personal twenty billion dollar Swiss account before the end of the year would become an illusion.

Oilgate International, after extensive meetings with him, had threatened to pull out of the country and sue the country in the International Court of Justice (ICJ). Oilgate was claiming there would be a breach of contractual agreement if an enabling environment were not provided.

The international community had unequivocally condemned the massacre of Tembeli indigenes during the peaceful rally. Ben Sare, in his address to the United Nations during World Environment Day, exposed the inhuman atrocities being perpetrated on Tembeli (a powerless ethnic minority) by Oilgate and the military government of Muzanga. He also exposed the environmental violations by Oilgate.

As Ben Sare stated, "Oilgate blatantly refused to deploy best industry practices in their oil exploration and production activities. There is an absence of genuine environmental impact assessment for projects, post-impact assessments for polluted lands, and bioremediation for heavily impacted lands."

Meanwhile, Ben Sare had toured about fifteen countries in Europe, Africa, and North America in an attempt to expose the environmental atrocities being committed by Oilgate.

The ninety-day notice given by Tembeli Liberation Movement was still in force, and if the situation was not adequately handled, it could lead to bizarre consequences.

"The nation is indeed sitting on powder keg," the HOS muttered again under his breath. He inhaled his cigarette once more and stepped out of the sitting room.

*   *   *

About a quarter of an hour later, the HOS arrived at the venue of the emergency meeting of the national ruling council. He was dressed in his full military regalia. The look on his face was anything but friendly.

As he entered the conference room, other military officers in attendance got to their feet to salute him. In attendance were chief of army staff, General Usman Aliyu; chief of air staff, General Musa Bantu, chief of naval staff, General Mustapha Lawal; and chief of defense staff, General Ali Usman.

The meeting was being held behind closed doors. Members of the press were barred from covering the event, and no communiqué was expected to be issued at the end of the meeting.

*   *   *

The time was 5:30 p.m. Tamuna's hostel, Hostel A, was buzzing with human activity. Every student was getting ready for sports.

Tamuna put on a pair of white shorts, a white T-shirt, and a pair of white canvass to match. Next, he opened his locker, took out his tennis racket (a present from Anita), and ran his fingers through it.

Tamuna enjoyed playing lawn tennis more than other games because he felt like it sharpened his sense of concentration and alertness.

He surveyed his racket once more and walked toward the door and out of the hostel. Midway through the path that led out of the hostel, Tamuna remembered that he had wanted to see Dagogo. Although there were a few Tembelites in Tembeli International School, Tamuna stuck more to Dagogo than others—probably because they had a similar background. Dagogo was one year below Tamuna, though.

Dagogo had earned a place in TIS on merit just like Tamuna. Dagogo was an introvert. He rarely spoke unless others spoke to him. There was always a thick, enigmatic aura around him that would otherwise make him less attractive to people . . . but for his soccer skills.

Tamuna wanted to engage Dagogo regarding the recent developments in Tembeli. When Tamuna reached Dagogo's hostel, he couldn't be found. He had left for the soccer field. Dagogo played defense on the school's soccer team.

"Hi Gogo," Tamuna shouted when he spotted Dagogo on the sideline.

"Aren't you playing today?" Tamuna asked.

"No, I am down with a knee injury. In fact, I have been out of action for two weeks now," Dagogo replied.

"So how does it feel to watch another play your position?" inquired Tamuna.

"Well, it is quite frustrating. All you do is try to find a fault in the person's pattern of play," Dagogo said.

"How about losing one's position to someone else as a result of injury?" Tamuna asked further.

"Oh! Man, that's the worst case scenario. No one ever wants to get to that spot."

"So try and get well quick!" Tamuna said.

"I am dead sure that, next week, I will bounce back into action to thrill my numerous fans once again with my mesmerizing soccer skills," Dagogo said before looking at Tamuna and saying, "I forgot to ask you one thing, Tam: why are you not properly dressed?"

Tamuna quickly looked over his clothing and replied, "How do you mean, Gogo?"

"What I mean is, this is a soccer field. Yours is not the correct attire for soccer!"

"Oh come off it, man!" Tamuna said, "You guys don't know how it feels to slam away in a court, do you?"

"Neither do you know how it feels to mesmerize fans with dribbling runs," Dagogo chipped in. They both roared with laughter.

"Well, Gogo, I came to see you for something very important," Tamuna started, "Can we have a little chat somewhere away from the crowd?" Tamuna led Dagogo away from the soccer field and toward the lawn tennis court.

They spotted a quiet place at the spectators' stand and sat down. There was a moment of silence. Tamuna broke the silence by asking, "Did you hear of the killings back home a fortnight ago?"

"Yes, I did," Dagogo answered, May the souls of our fallen heroes rest in peace. Amen."

"Gogo, have you paused to ask yourself why innocent people should be massacred for asking for their rights, for wanting to have a little share in what the Creator has blessed them with? Tell me: what is wrong with somebody crying out when he is oppressed?"

"I tell you, brother, that I broke my knee on the field after the massacre. Ever since, I have lost interest in almost everything around me. I want to read at times, but I find myself battling for hours to regain my concentration. A member of my family could have been killed. I just wish I could sneak out of school and rush back home," Dago ended.

"Gogo, Oilgate and the government are determined to see all of us dead," Tamuna said.

"They will definitely pay very soon," Dagogo added.

"Did you know my father was shot in the stomach?" Tamuna asked.

"Your father?" Dagogo asked in astonishment.

"But how do you know?" Dagogo continued.

"I participated in that rally. I narrowly escaped being shot dead," Tamuna said.

Dagogo regarded Tamuna briefly. He was both confused and amazed, and he said, "You are an enigma, Tam."

"Gogo, my reason for calling on you was not to talk about what happened; rather, I want us to assist in the liberation struggle."

Chapter Seven

His Excellency got up from his revolving chair where he had spent the greater part of the morning and moved toward the bar. He poured himself a drink. He took a sip and walked back to his chair. He lit a cigarette. His mobile phone rang, and he picked up the phone. It was Musa Garba, the petroleum minister.

"Why did you keep me in suspense?" the HOS asked.

"Sorry, Your Excellency. I just finished presiding over a meeting."

"Musa, what is the figure right now?" the HOS asked.

"Um, um, Your Excellency . . ." stammered Musa Garba.

"Look, while you ponder on the figure, bear in mind that it must hit twenty billion dollars before the end of the year!" the HOS shouted. The line went dead.

His Excellency pressed a combination of numbers on his mobile phone, and the finance minister, Professor Nnamdi Okeke was on the line.

"It is going to be very tight for the national economy very soon," the minister said. "Already, our crude has lost five dollars in the international oil market, and if this continues, our national fate seems uncertain,"

"Professor Okeke, that is not what I want to hear. Ensure that your figures are not embarrassing to the federal military government. The situation in Tembeli will soon be under control."

"Your Excellency, were it not for the nation's external debt of fifty billion dollars, the effect of the falling oil price would not have—" Again, the line went dead. The HOS was always irritated when reminded of the nation's debt.

The national ruling council's meeting the previous day had stretched over twenty hours. It was one stormy session after another. In the end, everybody was exhausted due to the mental gymnastics. Nevertheless, they arrived at a far-reaching consensus on interim measures concerning the wrangling in Tembeli Kingdom.

It was unanimously agreed among the national ruling council that some battalion from the 2nd Artillery Brigade of Muzanga Army should be temporarily camped some kilometers away from the troubled Tembeli Kingdom for emergency operations. The special operations group of the national mobile force would need to be specially equipped for combat readiness and prepared to await further instructions.

Meanwhile, the leader of the revolutionary movement in Tembeli Kingdom, Ben Sare, needed to be arrested and quizzed about his involvement in national sabotage. In general, key members of the liberation movement had to be closely monitored to avoid unpleasant surprises.

* * *

The morning dailies captured the most relevant issue of the moment: the arrest of Ben Sare, the leader of the Temebli Liberation Movement. A handful of students of Tembeli International School, upon hearing the news, rushed to the newspaper stand for more detailed information.

Tamuna held a copy of *The Guardian* newspaper amid trembling hands. Dagogo stood by his side. According to the story, the liberator was picked up at his residence the night before by men suspected to be members of the Muzanga Security Organization (MSO). Ben Sare's attempt—according to family sources—to ascertain the real identity of the plainclothes security agents proved unsuccessful. They drove off with the liberator in a black jeep, and no further news was available at press time.

* * *

Anita got up and walked toward the main sitting room. Halfway through the corridor, she jerked to a halt.

"Stop!" her father shouted.

Anita looked around, but she didn't see her father or her mother. She remained frozen and listened.

"I say, stop that nagging of yours. The shopping has to be called off!" her father shouted.

"Not this year again!" her mother shouted back. You promised us a week's shopping visit to London. Did you not?" she asked. "So what are you telling me now? To call it off? Never!"

There was some moment's silence. Next, Anita heard her mum sobbing uncontrollably.

"Darling, try to be understanding. I am calling it off on safety grounds. A lot of uncertainties hang in the air. From the way things are in the country now, nobody knows what will happen next," her father said.

Her mother's sobbing became more intense. Anita knew her mother well: she had a strong will, and she exhibited weakness in character only rarely. She was not easily broken by problems or anxiety. Anita had been looking forward to the end of her third year in Senior Secondary School because she would travel to the United Kingdom for shopping with her mother and brother.

Ever since the tradition began six years ago, her mother had taken them to the United Kingdom for shopping at the end of almost every school session. The trip was aborted the previous year, however, for reasons only known to her father.

"I have already promised the children we would go this year," her mother said again amid violent sobs. "How do I explain this to them? I don't want to break their hearts," she concluded.

"All right, darling, you can go on the trip." At the sound of those reassuring words from her father, the mayor of Tembeli Kingdom, Anita clasped her hands together in happiness and tiptoed silently back to the children's sitting room.

The weekend had been a boring one for Anita. It was devoid of the usual visits to the city to exchange pleasantries with friends and acquaintances—probably due to the recent state of unrest in the kingdom.

Anita still found it difficult to believe that she was really an indigene of Tembeli, the oil-rich kingdom of the Niger Delta. Having been born and bred in the United Kingdom, Anita imbibed Western thoughts and ideas. When her father came back to the country after his sojourn in the United Kingdom (and was made mayor of Tembeli), the thought of going home to Africa had gladdened her heart. Although she had heard a lot of distorted stories about Africa, she was determined to find things out for herself.

Her experiences defied her expectations when they arrived home, however. They lived in a government reserved area, an area designated for expatriates and resource persons in the kingdom. The school she attended was meant for the children of expatriates and their kind.

Anita rebelled against being a day student at first because she wanted to go to boarding school like other students. She wanted the opportunity to interact with children from different classes in society. Her father opposed the idea. He bought a new Peugeot salon car for her, and he employed a driver to be at her beck and call.

Ever since that decision was made, her life became a chain of managed events. She was raised to believe that the people of Tembeli were hostile because they were ungrateful to the federal military government of Muzanga. She was made to believe that other students of lower parentage should be avoided. Her friends were chosen for her for fear she would get mixed up with children from "questionable" backgrounds.

At school, she found it difficult to make friends because she did not know the students' backgrounds very well. This bothered Anita, especially when she saw how freely other students interacted with one another.

The satellite musical television channel was parading top pop artists, and Anita's siblings had their eyes glued to the TV. Although Anita sat and watched the musicals with them, her thoughts were running wild. Her mind drifted back to the first day, her first day at Tembeli International School. Her driver had dropped her off earlier than usual. She entered her class and met a group of three students who chatted happily with one another. She walked up to them, greeted them casually, and inquired whether the classroom was for freshmen like herself. In place of an answer, there was a roar of laughter. She was embarrassed by their conduct, and she walked to a quiet part of the room and sat down. She regarded them suspiciously.

"What else did you expect me to do, man?" one of them was saying. "She spoke through her nose. Didn't she?" he asked and roared with laughter once more.

"That wasn't fair. The fact that you didn't understand her intonation shouldn't call for ridicule," one of them retorted.

"Okay, mister nice guy," replied the third, "but even if she is a 'been to,' she must learn to speak properly."

"You guys amuse me. Here is a school, set apart for special people like her, you, and me. The fact that you earned a place here calls for a change in culture and subsequent adaptation to the new environment. Let me tell you something: walk up to that girl now and apologize for your rude conduct."

The last speaker had impressed Anita. And though the group talked like local kids, at least they seemed fairly civilized.

When his friends failed to apologize to Anita for their uncivilized behavior, one of the guys walked over to Anita and said, "Please don't mind my friends. They didn't mean to be rude."

"That's all right," she said.

"My friends call me Tam. My full name is Tamuna. I want you to call me Tam, too," he said.

Anita couldn't help smiling, and she said, "I am Anita."

That was about five years ago, and Tamuna had never stopped showing her that he was made of finer stuff than everybody else. The two of them remained very close acquaintances.

"Can I have the remote control, please?!" Anita's younger brother yelled. Anita was brought back to reality again.

Chapter Eight

Ben Sare opened his eyes. The room was so dark that he could not ascertain whether he was the only occupant. He wanted to get onto his feet, but he quickly changed his mind when he sensed that his entire body ached. It was as if a fifty kilogram load had been placed on top of him.

He eased himself into a sitting position and sat on the floor. The floor was cold, slimy, and slippery. Ben scanned the room. It was a small room, probably a small packing stall. There were no windows. The only source of illumination came from a single ray of light that streamed down from the high roof. Ben felt for his wristwatch. It was gone. He did not know what time it was, but he guessed it was about midday based on the single ray of light in the room that pierced the darkness like a sharp sword.

He tried to replay the events of the past few days in his mind. He had been gone for two days. No, three days—or was it four days? He had lost count after being abducted from his residence.

His abductors had stated that they were ordered to bring him in for interrogation. He wanted to resist the arrest, but he was overpowered by the men. He was bundled into a black jeep with a covered license plate. No sooner had the jeep left his residence—amid the screeching noise of tires—than two of the men blindfolded him with a thick black cloth. They also covered up his mouth. They twisted his hands behind his back and handcuffed him. They shoved him belly-up on the floor of the jeep and kicked him with their heavy boots.

Ben was left in great pain; his bones had been cracked beneath his frame. The jeep raced off for an indefinite amount of time. All Ben knew was that the jeep made a series of turns, stopped momentarily, and started back to life.

After what seemed like a twenty-four-hour journey, the jeep came to a final halt. Ben was again taken out of the jeep and led to an unknown destination. His abductors spoke no words. All Ben heard was the sound of boots. They stomped loudly and continuously, as if a battalion of soldiers were marching to the battle field. Ben simply followed his abductors.

At last, they stopped. A door was unlocked, and Ben was led into what seemed like a very long corridor. The entire place smelled of rotten feces and urine. Noise of varying frequencies tickled his ears as he passed through the corridor. And then they stopped. A door was unlocked. Screaming and other chaotic noises greeted him. He was carried inside, and the handcuffs were taken off his wrists. The door was locked again, and his abductors left him.

The rich smell of stool and urine permeated his nostrils. He loosened the pieced of cloth around his eyes and mouth and froze. He was in a cell. He scanned the room: there were five occupants in the cell. The youngest of them was an eighteen-year-old guy. He was so tall that his long frame seemed to hang loosely on his bones. He looked very sickly and hungry. He walked very slowly toward Ben. The other occupants simply watched the scene about to take place.

"Wetin be your name?" the lanky fellow queried in pidgin English, staring down at him.

Ben Sare was unsure what to make of the youth. He did not see it coming. And then, like a blinding flash of lightning, a mean slap went straight across Ben's face. He staggered, but he maintained his balance.

"Look, you bastard! Do you know what you have just done? You slapped me? Do you know who you slapped?" Ben shot back.

For an answer, there was a roar of laughter in the room.

"I say wetin be your name?" the boy asked again.

Ben stared at him, confused.

"Okay, wetin you bring come?" he asked.

"Look, for here, I be presido. When I talk, no one disobeys." he stated and laughed mischievously.

He took a step toward Ben. Even at the age of about fifty, Ben was convinced he could give the small brat a stiff challenge, so he stepped backward and prepared to attack. *Bam!* A violent strike came and stung his left ear dead.

"Oh!" Ben moaned, and he turned to behold another man who was short, very stout, and about twenty-five. The fellow had a menacing look in his eyes.

"Answer him," he grumbled in a croaky voice. Ben Sare turned to the lanky fellow, but was immediately swept off his feet from behind. He hit the ground with a big thud.

"Sit there, you idiot. If you get up, I go jus' blow your head!"

The fellow who spoke was the most muscular fellow Ben had ever seen. The man remained seated, though.

Ben complied like an obedient boy. He was being humiliated by hoodlums not even qualified to be his house help.

They searched him for money, but in the end, they were greeted with disappointment. There was not a dime on him.

"So you look us finis, think say na sand we dey chop. Abi? You wan' show us sey you get sense?" the bull queried. The lanky fellow waved the bull to a halt.

"Presido, no, I wan' teach an some small sense," the bull protested. The lanky fellow again stepped forward and stopped him.

"I don' see say you nefa know whey you dey. I go tell you," the lanky fellow said.

"Wetin be your name?" he asked.

Ben kept quiet and regarded him angrily.

"Na me you dey look like that?" the lanky fellow queried.

"Let us give this man VIP treatment," the lanky fellow ended.

"Okay, presido," the bull answered.

The bull dragged Ben to his feet and pinned his hand behind his back until it ached.

"Kabaka," the lanky fellow called.

"Presido," the short, stout man answered and positioned himself in front of Ben, awaiting for instructions.

"You don enter the lion den," the lanky fellow said and spat into Ben face.

"Fire!" he shouted. The stout man started to throw powerful punches at Ben. His face, his chest, his stomach—his whole body was besieged by blows coming in quick succession. Ben gasped for breath. His feet could no longer support his weight. He began to sag beneath his weight. The short fellow punched and kicked with reckless abandon.

Ben shouted and begged the others to come to his rescue, but it was to no avail. When they finally released him, he slumped to the floor and passed out.

*   *   *

Ben's eyes scanned the room once more and rested on the single ray of light from the roof. He shook his head as he remembered how he was brought to the second cell. Gradually, his eyes adapted to the semi-darkness, and the outline started to become distinct. When he realized that he was the sole occupant of the cell, he shrugged.

"Where are those bastards," he grumbled and cursed under his breath.

With extreme difficulty, he got to his feet. He limped around the room and felt the door knob. As he expected, it was locked. It was a steel door.

Ben sat down again on the slimy floor. He thought about the cause he stood for: total emancipation of his people from the shackles of environmental-induced slavery. It was his wish that other officials of the liberation movement used his absence to mobilize the people. He wanted the people to be on the alert for what would come next. The government was using its military might to induce fear in the Tembelites. Ben knew the military government would not be so naive as to attempt to kill him. He had established great confidence in the might of the international community—he knew they could ostracize the military government of Muzanga if he were killed.

It was not that the military government cared about fundamental human rights or wanted him alive; rather, the military government couldn't afford to gamble with the international outcry that would accompany Ben's sudden death.

There was a sound of approaching footsteps. The footstep ended at the door of Ben's cell. The lock was tried, and after a brief moment of fidgeting with the lock, the door was thrown wide open. Three men stepped into the cell. They shut the door behind themselves. They held pistols in their hands, and one of them held a flashlight.

The fellow who held the flashlight switched it on. The light momentarily blinded Ben Sare's eyes. One of them spoke in a quiet and calm voice: "We know who you are. We will not hurt you if you comply with our directives. Do not bother about our identity—it is not important."

Ben listened without uttering a single syllable, and the voice began again: "We want you to do one thing: denounce your leadership of the liberation movement. Do this, and you will regain your freedom."

"I do not speak with strangers. I should know the identity of whomever I am talking with. If you do not mind, introduce yourselves," Ben said.

"Like I said previously, our identities are not important."

"Who are your working for? What exactly do you want from me?" Ben asked in quick succession.

"Good, you are being very cooperative now. Simply say you do not wish to be involved with the liberation movement or cause any further confusion. Only then will freedom be yours."

Almost simultaneously, something clicked in the darkness. Ben was not a newcomer to this kind of game. He knew that the conversation was being taped.

"Gentlemen," he started, "I want you to know one thing: no degree of intimidation will ever make me disassociate myself from a cause I nurtured, cause which I have vowed to defend with the last drop of my blood. No amount of threatening whatsoever will make me denounce the movement that stood for hope in the midst of tutelage.

"What do you call freedom? I ask you gentlemen. Being released from a security cell and into a world in which you are enslaved for the rest of your life? A world in which you do not have a say in what concerns you? A world in which the future is bleak? No! I want you to tell me," Sare ended.

In answer, the man who had been speaking with him—apparently a leader of some sort—clapped his hand several times and smiled. "Good lecture, indeed," he said. "This is not an academic environment, my friend. This is a time that calls for serious business. Your liberty is in your own hands. Do not abuse this golden opportunity, for it may not come your way again. Are you willing to comply or not?"

Ben said nothing. There was silence.

"Mr. liberator—or whatever you think you are—why are you sabotaging the nation? Are you aware that your actions and those of your movement are detrimental to the economic well-being of Muzanga? Do you know that you are causing Muzanga a huge loss in revenue due to your clandestine activities?" The questions came in quick succession.

Ben chuckled and blurted out, "You guys are not competent enough to interrogate me. Besides, I do not even know what cause you stand for. Be bold enough to reveal your identity, and we shall talk."

"I have tried to be nice to you, but you seem to be playing the hero. I tell you once more: you will regret failing to comply with me," the man said and stepped backward.

The man who held the torch stepped forward and held Ben by the collar of his shirt. He yanked him upwards—inches off the floor—and released him. Ben slumped on the floor, lifeless. The three fellows exchanged glances and left the room, locking the door behind themselves.

Chapter Nine

Tamuna opened the main entrance door to the school's administrative block and walked in. He turned to his right and walked down the corridor. He was heading to Mr. Jack's office, which was located on the right side of the corridor.

He reached the door and tapped softly on it. He waited for some moments to elapse before pushing the door open. Mr. Jack stood by the window, looking out at the school's library. He had his back to the door when Tamuna entered.

"Good morning, sir," Tamuna said in greeting.

"Good morning!" Mr. Jack replied, "Please sit down." He motioned him to a seat and sat down in his own chair so he could face Tamuna. He held the day's copy of *The Guardian* newspaper.

"Have you read the paper today?" Mr. Jack asked.

"No, sir," Tamuna replied.

"Have a look at this," he said and passed the newspaper to Tamuna. He clasped his hands and watched as Tamuna scanned through the news items on the front page.

The caption simply read: "Military Government Accused of Abducting Ben Sare."

According to the story, the military government of Muzanga was alleged to be responsible for the abduction and had knowledge of Ben Sare's whereabouts.

In a press statement released on the previous day, deputy president of the liberation movement, Mr. Moses Kpandei, unequivocally stated that the abduction was a ploy aimed at not only diverting public opinion from the ninety-day ultimatum given to Oilgate International, but also sought to create panic and confusion among the union members.

The deputy president reaffirmed the union's commitment to abolishing the environmental atrocities committed by Oilgate International and the military government of Muzanga.

In another story on the front page—titled, "Government Denies Knowing the Whereabouts of Ben Sare"—the government's spokesman said the government was determined to unravel the mystery behind the disappearance of Ben Sare. He was also quoted as saying that it was wrong for citizens to insinuate the government's involvement. He stated that it was a machination of some foreign nations who claimed to love our dear country more than us. He was also quoted as saying that the police had been mobilized to unravel the mystery.

On the back page, Tamuna read the following caption: "United Nation Reacts to the Disappearance of Ben Sare."

Evidently, the United Nations condemned the alleged government abduction of the nation's foremost environmental activist, Mr. Ben Sare. The United Nations warned of imminent sanctions on the military government if human rights records were not improved.

Tamuna heaved a sigh of relief and looked up from the newspaper.

Mr. Jack cleared his throat and said, "Tamuna, I called you here to sample your views on the current state of events in your kingdom. Although I have been following the events as they unfolded, I have waited for a sign to appear."

"What sign are you talking about, sir?" Tamuna asked.

"I shall tell you in no distant time. First, bare your mind to me."

Tamuna's tongue went loose and he said: Ever since I was a child, I have had just one dream: to champion the cause of my people, a people gradually being driven into extinction because of a gift nature lavished upon them. I came to this school to arm myself with knowledge before stepping out into the turbulent environment of resistance. I have been wondering if—"

Mr. Jack sat still and waited for Tamuna to finish his speech. Soon after, Mr. Jack said, "Young man, this is not the time for oratory—this is the time for action. Tamuna, the sign is here." Mr. Jack paused again and observed Tamuna's reaction. "I am talking about the sign that will herald your making an inroad into the liberation movement," Mr. Jack finally said.

Tamuna stared at Mr. Jack in amusement. *What is this guy talking about?* he wondered, *Is he suggesting he is going to abandon his studies to join the resistance movement? This must be a joke.*

"Tamuna, ever since I came in contact with you, I have not doubted your potential. There is a vacuum that you must fill, and the time is now. The absence of Ben Sare in the liberation movement has created a vacuum—a dangerous vacuum. Your timely intervention will do the magic," Mr. Jack said. He smiled affectionately at Tamuna, and Tamuna stared back in confusion.

"Sir, I still have two semesters to go before bagging my senior secondary certificate. Are you suggesting I drop out of school and join the liberation struggle? Do you not know that there are other vibrant activists within the liberation movement?" Tamuna asked.

"Now listen attentively: I am neither suggesting you drop out of school nor suggesting that you take up the leadership of the liberation movement. What I'd rather suggest is that you spearhead the birth of a new movement—a youth wing of the liberation movement. You can operate undercover in the meantime. Anytime you want to sneak out of school, I will always provide the cover you need."

"The first semester holidays are around the corner, so you can use your spare time to consolidate your strategies. After the senior secondary certificate examinations (while you wait for your result), you will have all the time in the world to inject the much-needed vigor into the movement."

Tamuna sat and listened. *His brainwaves have been sent on an errand. This man has got lots of brains,* he thought.

"But you will always have one thing in mind: you must not forget your books. You must come succeed with flying colors on your final examinations—only then can you qualify to sit for university matriculation examination," Mr. Jack said.

Tamuna smiled and shook his head in affirmation as Mr. Jack continued: "That is why I called you to my office. You may have a contrary view, but I will want you to think about what I have said. Whenever you make up your mind, come back and tell me. I will give you the necessary tips to go about it." And then Mr. Jack got up from his seat, signaling the end of the meeting.

Tamuna got up too, thanked Mr. Jack, and left the office. Once outside—as he headed for his classroom—his favorite song, "Tomorrow," came to his lips. He sang it softly.

We shall sing with joy
Clapping and dancing
We shall walk freely about
With no sign of oppression
We shall be masters of our fate
When tomorrow comes
We shall bathe in the rivers
Without fear of contamination
We shall breathe the air
So pure and natural
We shall know when it's night
When tomorrow comes
We shall ask and receive
Like the scripture says
We shall seek and find
What is rightly ours
We shall knock and enter
When tomorrow comes

Chapter Ten

Ben Sare found himself in a state in between consciousness and unconsciousness—akin to the period of time when a fading dream gradually fuses with reality. He was conscious of the murmurs of people, the hustle and bustle of the street, the distant wailing of a police siren. He was conscious of many things, but he remained as still as a corpse. When at last he opened his eyes and stirred, a large shout of jubilation went into the air. It was only then that he became conscious of the drama—and the fact that he was the major actor.

He lay close to a heap of rubbish near the road. A crowd was gathered all around him. Pressmen had a field day poking their microphones in different directions, wanting to catch the news item of the moment.

Television crews were equally busy flashing their cameras in different directions. The once distant wailing of the police siren closed in. A fierce-looking team jumped out of the police jeep and tore through the crowd. They reached the spot where Ben Sare was lying—still bound at his hands and feet—and freed him. Next, they put him into a police car and drove off at top speed. The efforts of the press to get the police chief to make some comments on the issue proved abortive because he said he was not able to make any official statement.

*   *   *

Tamuna arrived home at about six o'clock in the evening. He received a warm embrace from his parents. His younger sister and brother were overjoyed at the sight of him. However, they wondered why he had come unannounced—they knew full well that holidays were still a few weeks ahead.

His father did not hide his feelings. After the usual exchange of pleasantries, he called Tamuna aside and whispered into his ears. He said, "My son, I hope all is well at school. My mind tells me there is something else about this visit of yours. Our people say that a toad does not run about in daylight for nothing."

"Papa, all is well at school. I came for a purpose, a special mission that I must accomplish before tomorrow evening," Tamuna replied.

"What mission?" Ledum queried.

"Papa," Tamuna started, "the young people of this great kingdom are appreciative of the role that you (our parents) are playing to end our strife. This kingdom belongs to all of us, though. And we believe—with the learning we have—that we will add another feather to the cap of the liberation movement."

"Papa, do not misunderstand me. What I mean is that, back at school, though we are a small group, we have agreed to support the struggle by forming a youth movement. It will be under the control of the liberation movement, and it will provide the wood with which the flames of the struggle will be fed. I was actually mandated to go home and sell the idea to the youth throughout the kingdom of Tembeli."

"Hmm, I am happy. All of you at school have not forgotten your roots. I am indeed pleased that you have not forgotten the plight of your people. You are the seeds that will germinate and bring forth the fruits of tomorrow. I give you my blessing. May the Almighty God protect and guide you in all your deliberation," Ledum stated.

Tamuna went about his task of mobilizing the youth with vigor. He went from house to house, and he was assisted by his younger brother, who had more access to the youth in the village.

By the time, it was ten o'clock at night, a sizable number of young people from the village (and delegates from other villages in the kingdom) had gathered at the village square for the emergency meeting.

Tamuna stood up among the group and spoke: "My brothers, may I first apologize for disturbing your peace at this time of night. But tell me, what peace has a man whose house is on fire? No peace, indeed. The way you responded to this call makes me happy. It shows that this great kingdom can still boast of young men who have love for the land that gave them birth.

"All of us here are living witnesses to the suffering in the land and the efforts to free us all from the agents of oppression. The military government is determined to have Oilgate continue their oil production in Tembeli because it is the oil that makes their pockets fat.

"We are not saying, 'Don't produce oil'; rather, we are saying, 'Let us have a fair share of the oil that is being drilled in our land so that we can use the revenue to rewrite the history of our kingdom.'" What we are saying is, 'Do not make our lands sterile and uninhabitable after oil production; do not turn our sons and daughters into shooting targets; do not endanger our livelihood.'

"Back at school, we have organized ourselves into a small group with a mandate to go back home and tell our brothers in the village that now is the time for the youth to raise their voices. It is time to tell Oilgate International and the military government of Muzanga that they can harass Ben Sare and other leaders of the liberation movement, that they can capture and detain all the leaders of the movement, but the movement lives on!

"We have to organize ourselves into a vigilante group whose activities will be secret and supportive to the aims of the liberation movement. That is our role, and that is why I was asked to come and tell you this," Tamuna said and sat down.

His speech captivated the youth. As soon as he sat down, a murmur of approval interrupted the stillness of the night. One after the other, the delegates spoke. They all expressed their views on the issue. They all expressed their unalloyed support for the formation of the clandestine body. One youth, however, was critical of the birth of the new body.

His name was Bari, and he was popular in the village for his critical views on issues. They called him the man with a third eye. Bari, while maintaining that he was in support of the formation of the new group, expressed a number of fears. He wanted to know the real function of the new body as a supportive arm of the liberation movement. Also, he wanted to know the operational limits of the new body; he wanted to know whether the parent body was aware of the formation of the new body; he wanted to know into whose hands the leadership of the group would be entrusted. He wanted to know many things."

When he sat down, there were grumbles of disapproval. Although Bari was noted for his critical stance on issues, in most cases his criticism had proved to be instrumental to the success of projects that had been carried out in the kingdom.

When Tamuna stood up to respond to Bari's questions, he realized that young men with vibrant minds still abounded in Tembeli Kingdom. He knew he had set in motion a chain reaction that would ultimately lead to success.

Thanks to Mr. Jack, Tamuna thought, *for all the nitty-gritty details needed for the formation of the body. The information was given to me on a platter of gold.*

Tamuna thanked Bari for his contribution to the issue. He explained, however, that the task at hand belonged to all of them. He explained that each and every one of them should go home and think about some of the issues raised—no one was claiming to have more knowledge. He professed that, with a collective will and great determination, their dreams would eventually be realized.

He said he was sent out on an errand to solicit their support for a new body. He then urged them to think about the way forward.

The first crow from the cock was heard at dawn when the group rose to go. Tamuna was totally famished, and he wondered how he was going to cope with the stress back at school without a good night's sleep.

Chapter Eleven

Great fear and insecurity hung in the air within Tembeli Kingdom. Everybody woke up in the morning to behold the recent declaration of the military government. A dusk-to-dawn curfew throughout the kingdom was announced. Anybody caught contravening the order would be seen as government saboteurs.

The special operations group of the mobile police force had formed a joint patrol team with members of the 2nd Artillery Brigade. The type of ammunition they carried made one wonder whether such ammunition was going to be used on defenseless citizens or enemy comabatants.

Meanwhile, the deadline given to Oilgate International by the liberation movement had expired. Oilgate had made no genuine effort to negotiate the terms stated by the liberation movement, and they had gone on with their oil production activities. Their pipe-laying contractor had been asked to mobilize back to site and commence the laying of the eighty-kilometer pipeline linking one of the newly discovered oil wells to the flow station. The activities at the pipeline site were anything but dull. Any passerby might wonder whether Oilgate and the host community were involved in any kind of disagreement.

A special security network had been provided for Oilgate contractors and sub-contractors to avoid any surprises from the host community.

Production activities were also continuing in existing oil wells in Tembeli Kingdom—despite the refusal of Oilgate International to go to the negotiation table with the liberation movement.

The liberation movement had remained incommunicado, and their silence made both the military government and Oilgate International uneasy. Meanwhile, the Tamuna-led vigilante group had perfected all its strategies for the night. Two attacks had been penciled in for the night. The major flow station would be shut down, and the structures would be set ablaze. Second, the camp belonging to Oilgate contractors would be attacked and set on fire. These attacks were dubbed *Operation 001*.

The military government also shut down Tembeli International School. The government had alleged that some clandestine groups were getting together in the school under the auspices of some unidentified external union. These group were (allegedly) inciting the students to revolt against the government. Also, the government's allegation said a letter—purportedly from the liberation movement—threatened an attack on the school unless it was shut down.

Tamuna received the news of the indefinite closure of Tembeli International School with mixed feelings. He now had a tremendous opportunity: he could nurse his baby vigilante organization. Though it was true that Tamuna had not yet taken his school certificate examinations or the university matriculation examination, he knew he had to liberate his people first.

After a series of meetings with the youth in the kingdom, it was agreed that Tamuna would lead a delegation to the leaders of the liberation movement to solicit support prior to the formation of the movement. Expectedly, the liberation movement was pleased that such an idea was coming from the youth. The vigilante movement was secretly inaugurated shortly after Tamuna and his peers went home for break.

The meeting and inauguration ceremony were incredible for Tamuna because he had the opportunity to meet the man of his dreams—the man with the pipe: Ben Sare, the liberator. The liberator expressed great joy that the liberation movement could count on youth of Tamuna's caliber to keep the flag of the liberation movement flying.

*   *   *

Two youngsters were selected to lead Operation 001 (OP001). Tamuna was at the head of the flow station attack group, and Bari (the man with the third eye) would lead the contractor campsite attack. The two operations were to be carried out neatly and simultaneously.

Members of the OP001 group were split up into groups of three. They set about reviewing their strategies in light of the security patrol team made up of the army and the mobile police. They kept reiterating that it was going to be a decisive but sensitive operation. The main arsenal at the disposal of the OP001 attack team was a host of petrol bombs, synthesized under the supervision of Ben Sare. Although Ben was placed under house arrest, he frequently sneaked out of his home through a tunnel in his wardrobe at about midnight to consult with members of the liberation movement and the vigilante group.

The attack was slated for two o'clock in the morning, and the group relaxed in their bush camp hideout, waiting for the zero hour.

*　*　*

The mayor of Tembeli Kingdom sat in his sitting room. The time was seven o'clock in the evening. The day had been boring—he spent his time within the confines of his compound. Even with the beefing up of security around his residence, he still had a reason to panic.

Something within him kept saying that a day would come when he would become a target of the liberation movement. His antiliberation stance would be called into question. But of course, he had to dance to the tune of those who made him mayor of Tembeli Kingdom, the oil-rich kingdom of the

Niger Delta. He poured himself a glass of brandy and sipped it nervously.

The entrance door creaked slowly. The mayor jumped up from his settee, spilling the remainder of the brandy on his clothes.

"Daddy! Daddy!" his youngest child—about two years old—shouted as he limped toward him with outstretched arms.

"Shit!" the mayor yelled as he relaxed to take the kid into his arms. The child put up one or two playful acts, but upon sensing that his father was not interested in play, he burst into tears. The child's cries attracted the attention of his mother.

"What has come over you, Isaac?" his wife queried as she gathered the crying child in her arms.

"Can't you sooth a crying child anymore? Do you mean to tell me that you did not hear the baby's cry?" she quizzed further.

For an answer, the mayor took a sip from his brandy and picked up his copy of *The Guardian* newspaper. His wife sighed and walked briskly out of the sitting room, cradling her child to her bosom. She shut the door with a big bang that made the mayor jump up again from his settee.

"Shit! Shit!" he blurted out, and he tried to steady his nerves.

The first heading on the front page read as follows: "Tembeli: A Time Bomb Waiting to Explode." It made him even more nervous.

The mayor read the article three times, and the more he thought about the news, the more adrenaline surged through his system.

According to the story, the military government of Muzanga had made no genuine effort to restore normalcy in Tembeli Kingdom. They had not taken the ninety-day deadline given by the liberation movement seriously. The story also said that, rather than initiate genuine reconciliation, the military government had placed the leader of the liberation movement under house arrest, prevented him from seeing a doctor, placed a dusk-to-dawn curfew on Tembeli, and put fierce-looking mobile policemen and soldiers on alert throughout the kingdom.

The government had evidently adopted a new strategy: arresting some of the key members of the liberation movement on the grounds that they constituted a security risk. The latest move, according to the story, was made to further paralyze the liberation movement. The government was blamed for blatantly oppressing people who were being rendered powerless (and whose only crime was asking for what rightly belonged to them).

Chapter Twelve

Tamuna rolled from side to side on the wooden floor. He propped his head on his palms after planting his elbows on the wooden floor. His head ached.

He looked around, and a twist of a smile formed on his lips. The other five guys were still fast asleep even though it was already morning. Tamuna did not know what time it was—he lost his wrist watch during the previous night's operation.

The operation had been successful; it had been executed simultaneously as planned. Within thirty minutes (after two o'clock in the morning), the flow station was in flames. The blackness of the smoke emanating from the ruins mingled with the night and cast dark shadow against the dim light pulsing from the oil flare torches.

It had not been easy for Tamuna and his crew to beat the very tight security network at the flow station. Their bombs had struck the right targets, though, and fires had erupted. They had waited for the fire to cause the desired panic. The emergency alarm at the flow station had been triggered, and personnel were seen running out to the muster station. In the confusion of the moment, they had escaped.

While the flow station was in flames, Bari and his crew struck the Oilgate contractor camp, and the effect was amazing. They had been very careful to hit low density areas—their mission was not to cause the loss of life, it was to create panic and confusion.

Tamuna got to his feet and paced around the makeshift camp. The structure was suspended in the swamp by logs of timber extending on either side. The floor was made of smaller logs that were constructed and joined so closely as to present a floor-like appearance. Raffia palm leaves were used as roofing structures, and they were hung on the four sides of the structures.

The camp had been constructed right in the middle of the dying, swampy mangrove forest of Tembeli. The mangrove vegetation bordering the camp, although sickly in appearance, still provided the much-needed cover for members of the OP001 squad. The camp could only be reached with specially designed canoes paddled by unusually skilled individuals.

No security network, no matter how observant, would be able to detect the camp easily. The boys felt secure in their swampy camp.

Tamuna looked across the vast expanse of the swamp and wondered what the whole place would have looked like in an ideal state. The forest would have been very lush with birds and animals having a field day. From a distance, he heard the sharp shrill of a bird's voice. The bird jumped and hopped from one dying tree to another as if protesting the powers that had driven away animal life from the once-bubbling, swampy mangrove forest.

Tamuna's thoughts ran wild as he considered Tembeli Kingdom. He could not suppress the droplets of tears that formed in his eyes.

"Never!" Tamuna shouted. He had allowed his emotions to take control of him. He had stamped his foot against a wooden structure near him. The structure shook. Bari opened his eyes, murmured some incoherent syllables, and went back to sleep immediately.

*   *   *

The nation awoke that morning to behold one of the worst disasters to hit the oil industry. The biggest flow station of Oilgate International was on fire. The attack, according to government sources, was supposedly carried out by members of the liberation movement. The entire security network of the government had been beaten thoroughly. In a swift action—as if to avenge their humiliation—the army and members of the mobile police force went on a rampage. They arrested and detained all men that they ran into. A total of twenty youngsters were shot dead when they resisted arrest, and several others were wounded while being arrested.

Tembeli Kingdom mourned its dead. There was great weeping throughout the land. Members of the liberation movement (including Ben Sare) who were already under house arrest were transferred to the maximum security detention camp of the 2nd Artillery Brigade.

The government spokesman said the liberation movement had formed a guerilla operation to spearhead the attacks. The liberation movement, however, had not claimed responsibility for the attacks. And no other groups claimed responsibility either.

The mayor of Tembeli, Honorable Isaac Birago, sat with the principal of Tembeli International School in his exquisitely furnished sitting room. Also seated with them was Honorable Briggs, the administrator of Tembeli. Their issue of discourse was the state of Tembeli Kingdom.

"It is my opinion that government is not tackling this issue intelligently," the principal said. "They are worsening an already worsened situation," he added.

"Are you suggesting they allow Ben Sare and his group to have their way?" the mayor asked.

"Much depends on what you mean by *having their way*," said Briggs, Look, the people were upset about something that affected their livelihood. They gave conditions that needed to be met. What prevented the government from instituting a panel of inquiry into their claims? Of course, you know the inquiry can last a year or two, depending on what the government has in mind. Afterward, they can invite the movement to a conference table for renegotiation. No matter how long it takes for a meaningful consensus to be reached, at least the world would see that some efforts were being made to address the situation. But look at what they did." Briggs sounded furious.

"But why the shootings? Were the shootings actually necessary at this stage?" the mayor asked.

"The army and the mobile police must have been under instructions to shoot on sight, otherwise they wouldn't have reacted the way they did," replied the principal.

"It is not that I am being pessimistic, but I think something very tragic is going to happen very soon," Briggs said, "The United Nations is already advocating economic sanctions against the nation, including a boycott of the nation's oil in the international market. If that happens, then we are in trouble!"

"I pray it doesn't escalate to that," the mayor said, "I believe the government will do something fast to diffuse the present tension in the land."

Chapter Thirteen

His Excellency and members of the highest ruling body of the nation rose from a ninety-six-hour emergency meeting held to find a lasting solution to the Tembeli crisis. It was agreed that the leader of the liberation movement, Ben Sare, should be released from detention and invited to negotiate with the government. The hope was to reduce the tension in Tembeli kingdom.

The climax of the meeting was the drafting of Dauda Ahmed of the special military intelligence unit to understudy the activities of the liberation movement and come up with a lasting solution to the crisis.

His Excellency was visibly shaken by the attack on the flow station. He needed no one to tell him that the liberation movement had orchestrated the attack, but one thing still baffled him: the attack was launched when Ben Sare was under house arrest, and he had ensured that trusted men were monitoring him day and night. *Could there be some conspiracy?* he wondered. The answers refused to come, but he wasted no time redeploying men to watch Ben Sare's residence.

The speculation that a guerilla movement had been formed by the liberation movement was still being investigated. If the outcome of the investigation was positive, he would have many more nuts to crack.

His Excellency lit a cigarette and poured himself a drink. He paced from one end of his conference room to the other, sending his brain waves on errand. He sat down and stubbed his cigarette in the ashtray. The ashtray was filled up, and ashes had started to drop onto the table. For the first time in a long time, the head of state came to the realization that he had exceeded his usual cigarette smoking rate.

*   *   *

Suddenly, there was a click on his mobile phone, and Dauda Ahmed literally jumped from the bed and grabbed it. "Hello, who's speaking?" he asked.

"Ahmed, something is wrong here," the voice of the head of state bellowed from the other end of the phone, "I want to speak with you alone. Do you have company?"

"Yes," Ahmed answered.

Ahmed took a leisurely stroll toward the sitting room, while still glued to his mobile phone. He cast a glance at Amina, who lay on the bed beside him. She looked terribly anxious and disturbed.

"Ahmed, the situation here is gradually getting out of hand. I believe you know what I am talking about."

"Yes, I do, Your Excellency: the Tembeli Kingdom crisis," he muttered.

"Right," His Excellency echoed, "Ahmed, I want someone very competent to handle the situation."

"But Your Excellency, there are lots of competent guys in the MIU who can handle the job perfectly," Ahmed said.

"Ahmed, you have to call off your vacation. I am expecting you back tomorrow evening," His Excellency ordered. The line went dead.

"Darling, what is the matter," Amina asked as Ahmed strolled back into the bedroom, visibly angry.

Ahmed gathered her in his arms and looked deeply into her pair of exquisite eyes. The words refused to form on his lips.

"Come on, darling, speak up. What is the matter with you? Who was that on the phone?"

Ahmed was sweating profusely from head to toe, and he replied, "We will call off our honeymoon."

"What? Are you crazy or something? What exactly did you say?" She shook loose from his embrace.

Ahmed picked up his pack of cigarettes, selected one, and lit it. He inhaled deeply and said, "Amina, I am sorry about this. You see, this is one of the numerous sacrifices that accompanies my job. My superior wants me back for an important assignment."

Amina broke into a sob and asked, "What kind of life is this? We only arrived last week, and you are telling me the honeymoon will be called off? Why can't they leave you alone for a moment?" She sobbed and sobbed. Ahmed was helpless; his attempts to soothe her proved abortive.

"Imagine what time it is," she said amid tears, pointing to the wall clock, "Even at midnight, they will not leave somebody alone!"

He reached for the phone and called the hotel reception for drinks. He sat in a settee and smoked a cigarette.

Since he joined the military ten years before, Ahmed had always been penciled in to handle cases that otherwise were deemed impossible. His first mission as a young officer—fresh out of school—was an espionage mission in Cuba. He was detailed to track down a famous drug cartel that used the nation as a transit point. All the other officers who were drafted to that project were either killed or captured by the drug syndicates. When Ahmed volunteered to be drafted into the espionage team, he didn't know it would be the beginning of a nightmare—a nightmare full of repeated mission. Not only was Ahmed able to uncover the cartel network of the drug baron, his input led to the eventual collapse of the entire drug business.

For Ahmed, it was one mission after the other. When he finished his last mission, a spying mission in Indonesia, he said it was high time to go on some vacations. He hurriedly got wedded to Amina, his sweetheart, and he requested a one-month vacation to enjoy his honeymoon. Little did he know that trouble would soon come knocking at his door.

Barely one week after Ahmed's arrival in New York City, His Excellency (the head of state and commander in chief of the Republic of Muzanga) urgently wanted him back home to handle yet another job reserved for people like him.

The door bell rang. Ahmed rushed for the door handle and opened it. The waiter entered with glasses of wine and placed them on the table. He left after murmuring some pleasantries. Ahmed drank one of the glasses and thought about the latest job on his hands.

*   *   *

As the clock struck 5:00 p.m., dusk began to descend on Liberation Square. From a distance, the smoky flames of Oilgate's gas flares could be seen polluting the atmosphere.

Liberation Square was packed full of people. Looks of disgust seemed to settle on most faces as they watched with disappointment as two rivals of the liberation movement engaged in a war of words. It was an act akin to the violent outpour of lava from a volcanic site. The two culprits in question were Ben Sare, the leader of Tembeli Liberation Movement and Mr. Jackson Bright, a minority leader in the liberation movement. The object of disagreement was a piece of paper that measured about fifteen centimeters by ten centimeters.

The head of state and commander in chief of the Republic of Muzanga had written to the leadership of the liberation movement. He had invited them to a peaceful negotiation aimed at finding a lasting solution to the feud in Tembeli Kingdom. In the letter (signed by the press secretary), His Excellency expressed dissatisfaction in the way in which the crisis was being managed. He stated, "It is my sincere wish that we put heads together to put an end to the crisis that has claimed the lives of the illustrious sons and daughters of this great nation."

When Ben Sare went to the presidential villa for negotiation, however, there was a stalemate. Ben said that, though he welcomed the olive branch being extended by the head of state, the government needed to convince global observers that their intentions were not malicious." He then gave the government a five-point list of conditions that had to be met before any meaningful negotiation could commence. The conditions were as follows:

1. Release all other executives of the liberation movement.

2. Release all detainees still held in government custody.

3. Demobilize all contractors of Oilgate carrying out pipeline-laying jobs (pending the resolution of the crisis).

4. Reduce flow station activity to fifty percent capacity.

5. Recall all members of the SOG of the mobile police force and army presently parading throughout Tembeli kingdom and let the police force handle law enforcement.

Because of the stalemate, Ben had summoned his people to tell them about the new developments. All but a small dissident group led by Jackson Bright agreed to the stand taken by Ben Sare. The Jackson Bright-led dissident group accused Ben of hijacking the liberation movement as a tool to launch himself into international prominence. They maintained that he not only took the entire glory of the liberation struggle, but also that he suppressed other activists in the movement. They claimed that he did not represent the interest of the entire kingdom. They maintained that if he did not commence negotiation with the government, Jackson Bright would lead a delegation of concerned Tembeli indigenes to the head of state for negotiation.

Ben Sare accused Jackson Bright of being insensitive to the plight of the teeming masses within Tembeli Kingdom because Jackson enjoyed one government contract after another. He accused Jackson of being an opportunistic activist whose sole aim was to sell the people to the government. Ben said that Jackson had a secret agenda and was bent on satisfying his selfish desire to become the next mayor of Tembeli Kingdom. The war of words continued.

*   *   *

Tamuna watched helplessly as chaos crept into a liberation movement that once stood for the dreams and aspirations of the teeming populace of Tembeli Kingdom. He had been ferried from the swampy camp to attend the crucial meeting as the leader of the youth movement there, and he knew that if Jackson Bright got his way, things would fall apart.

Chapter Fourteen

"Your Excellency, this is going to be the easiest job I have handled in my entire career," Ahmed Dauda said.

"What makes you think so," the HOS inquired.

"First, this guy Jackson is a complete charlatan. I have met his kind a couple of times. He does not seem smart."

"That makes it better for us," His Excellency said.

"Definitely, Your Excellency. With him and his newly formed movement working in opposition to the liberation movement, the success of my mission is as sure as death."

"If Jackson is made to have whatever he demands, we can use him to breed division and confusion in Tembeli Kingdom. The kingdom will turn against him. Ben Sare will turn against him, and the youth will want his head. It is no longer news that he and Ben Sare are archrivals. We can pay Jackson to mount incessant attacks on Ben Sare's leadership of the liberation movement. And then, if Jackson gets murdered, Ben Sare is off the scene. His exit, coupled with the present detention of other activists, will create a vacuum too big to fill in the liberation movement." The HOS nodded and said, "What an excellent plot."

"In just one week, Your Excellency, the job will be through. The nation will no longer be confronted with the so-called Tembeli Kingdom crisis."

The head of state got up from his revolving armchair. He fished inside his pocket and took out his handkerchief. He mopped his face and paced around the conference room. Although the air conditioner was set to the coldest temperature, the head of state was sweating profusely.

Ahmed Dauda's meeting with Jackson Bright a few hours before had provided him with the missing link he had been looking for. The HOS had insisted that Ahmed Dauda be present during the closed-door meeting.

"That seals it then," the HOS said and extended his hands to Ahmed Dauda, "Whenever you are ready to commence operations, you will have whatever you request."

"Thank you, Your Excellency, for yet another opportunity to serve. I will leave for Tembeli tomorrow evening."

"You are welcome," His Excellency said.

*   *   *

Jackson Bright, after leaving the presidential villa, gave a world press conference. The National Television Authority, the National Radio Corporation, and the international and local media organizations covered the event. He solicited the world's support in bringing the aggrieved and exploited people of Tembeli and the government of the Republic of Muzanga to the negotiation table.

He said, "In an atmosphere of rancor and acrimony, true negotiation becomes impossible." He claimed that he had the support of a large percentage of Tembeli indigenes who were yearning for a peaceful resolution to the crisis. He stated, "The people cried to me and said they were tired of bloodshed and fear, which had become a daily phenomenon in Tembeli Kingdom."

Jackson Bright accused Ben Sare of being unnecessarily confrontational, and he asked his rival to embrace true change.

He also called on the guerilla movement—allegedly formed by Ben Sare—to come out of the creeks and join his movement. He promised that his movement, The Movement of Concerned Tembeli Indigenes (MCTI), would liberate Tembeli Kingdom from oppression and herald the dawn of a new era for all Tembelites.

The Guardian newspaper, on its front page, noted the following: "The rivalry between Ben Sare and Jackson Bright is deepening."

Ben Sare described Jackson Bright as a man of revolutionary emptiness who was being used by the military government to divert the attention of the world from the real issues at hand. He said Jackson Bright was a government stooge whose selfish motives were aimed at blackmailing the activities of the liberation movement.

He warned the peace-loving citizens of Tembeli Kingdom to be careful when dealing with Jackson Bright, whom he described as a paid government spokesman who was hired to sow a seed of discord within the liberation movement.

*   *   *

All the youth of Tembeli Kingdom not part of the guerilla movement (who had survived being murdered, detained, or intimidated) were mourning. They were not mourning their compatriots who had lost their lives in the liberation struggle. They were not mourning the land that had been debased. They were not mourning the resources that were being forcefully removed. Rather, they were mourning someone who was still alive. They were mourning Jackson Bright.

The youth—numbering over one hundred thousand—marched through the streets of Tembeli in a macabre manner. They were all clad in black. They neither sang nor shouted. They all had pieces of palm fronds in between their lips. Many of them carried placards on which their feelings were conveyed. Some of the placards read as follows:

"We must resist attempts to blackmail our struggle!"

"Jackson Bright is a traitor, MCTI is a fake!"

"Jackson Bright, enough is enough!"

The youth started their procession in Liberation Square. They carried a black coffin, which they deposited in front of Jackson's house. They made no attempt to vandalize or loot any property belonging to him, however, They made no violent attacks on anybody; they simply marched silently.

The eagle-eyed mobile policemen (and the soldiers who were on the alert to shoot) were beaten by this manner of demonstration. They simply followed the youth wherever they want.

The press was there, and they had a field day. They captured all the exciting moments of the demonstration. Toward evening, after having visited almost all of Jackson Bright's converts, the procession marched to Liberation Square where they dispersed without ceremony.

*   *   *

That same evening, news was passed to Tamuna's leadership that the guerilla movement was going to shift its operational base from the creeks to the land. The leader of the liberation movement, Ben Sare, in a secret message, explained why he wanted such a change. According to him, a vacuum had been created in the movement by the continued detention of some of the key actors, and the need had arisen for an organized youth movement to fill the interim vacuum.

As Tamuna and his crew prepared to move back to the land, they could not help but think of a possible way out of the present, messy state of affairs.

"Tam, imagine all the effort that has been put into this struggle. And overnight, someone appears from nowhere and starts playing the spoiler," Bari said.

"Bari, what bothers me most is the fact that the government—in addition to using this fool called Jackson Bright to discredit our movement—may have a hidden agenda," Tamuna said.

"I agree with you. I pity Jackson Bright. If I could get hold of him, I would definitely crush his stupid skull," Bari said angrily.

"He is not going to make any headway. By the time he is used and dumped—if he is still alive—he will know what a mess he has landed himself into. Right now, he thinks he is the new messiah . . . but he should wait and see."

Chapter Fifteen

"There won't be any need for fanfare," Ahmed Dauda said.

"Why not," asked Jackson.

"You have to show all that you really mean business. That movement of yours is an action group committed to bringing a genuine resolution to the crisis at hand," Ahmed said.

"But the presence of the press is unavoidable," Jackson said.

"Of course they will be there, but you should be careful what you say to them. They are quite smart, you know."

Jackson nodded in acceptance.

"One more thing: I must not be mentioned to anybody—neither can I be seen with you. In fact, as far as this inauguration ceremony and other issues are concerned, I do not exist," Ahmed said.

"You do not *what?*" Jackson asked and burst into laughter.

"What is so funny? You don't seem to understand exactly what is going on," Ahmed said.

"What amuses me is the fact that the successes I have made in less than one week could not have been made without you. Don't you know? With your financial support, I have tamed lots of Ben Sare's loyalists. Did you know the membership has gradually swelled? And now you tell me you don't exist?"

"Man, what I am saying is, do not mention me to the press. Okay?" Ahmed barked. And then he grabbed Jackson by the collar of his shirt and shook him violently.

"I certainly understand." Jackson murmured with fright.

"I wish you a successful inauguration. You will have adequate security backing. I leave tonight. As I told you, whatever further assistance you need, you will receive, I will see you in your hotel room tonight, just before I leave," Ahmed said and smiled. They shook hands. Ahmed Dauda left the lobby and moved toward the staircase and toward his hotel room. Jackson Bright stormed out of the hotel and into the street.

*   *   *

Ahmed Dauda, upon arrival in Tembeli Kingdom five days earlier, had been a participant of many meetings, all of them secretly arranged. He wielded great popularity within the military cycle because his presence stood for one thing: success. Whatever assistance he needed was always given to him immediately. Thus, when he met with the officer commanding the 2nd Artillery Brigade and solicited his assistance, all assistance was assured him. His meeting with the head of operation of the special operations squad of the mobile police force also ended on a positive note. Both officers reaffirmed their dedication to him and the head of state.

Ahmed Dauda's support of Jackson had been impressive. With just a few days until the formal inauguration of Jackson's Movement for Concerned Tembeli Indigenes, the whole kingdom was charged with fear due to the chain of events triggered by Jackson's actions. Liberation Square, the venue of the inauguration, was wearing a bright look. There were decorations scattered about. Heavily armed mobile policemen were seen idling away, not harassing anybody. Their presence, without a doubt, frightened the peace-loving citizens of Tembeli Kingdom.

A few of Jackson's converts could be seen putting finishing touches on the kick-off ceremony. Their faces indicated happiness and confidence, which suggested that they had stolen the show from Ben Sare's liberation movement.

Somewhere within the town, a secluded spot some kilometers from his residence, Tamuna was busy giving out instructions to a group of youngsters, leaders of the guerilla movement. Bari was there; Dagogo was there. In fact, all the young men of substance in the kingdom were present.

As they listened to Tamuna's ideas about how to publicly protest against the formation of Jackson's movement, their minds were set for the worst. Tamuna told them not to allow sentiments to control them. They were instructed to conduct themselves peacefully and responsibly. He reiterated the need for all to lay down their lives in order to see the eventual success of the cause.

*   *   *

There were many people in Liberation Square, the venue for the formal inauguration ceremony of the MCTI. This was disappointing because Ben Sare had (for days) campaigned, urging people to boycott the inauguration ceremony. The mobile police patrolled the arena, looking as fierce as ever.

The ceremony was very peaceful, though. The press had a field day, and they flashed their cameras and poked their microphones with reckless abandon. Jackson was undoubtedly the man of the moment. All attempts made by the press to get Jackson to say a few words, however, yielded no fruit.

A few of Jackson's loyalists were on the wooden rostrum that had been erected on Liberation Square. Each of them was given an opportunity to say a few things to the crowd. After each speech, a round of clapping usually followed. There was great expectation and anticipation as the crowd cheered one speaker after another. The crowd still waited for the big moment, though—the moment when Jackson would mount the rostrum.

A short distance away, by the road that led into Liberation Square, a small crowd was slowly making their way into the square. The crowd consisted of youth, both male and female. They were chanting solidarity songs and dancing to the rhythm of the martial tune. They were members of the youth wing of the liberation movement. As they approached, they were not spotted. Gradually, they made their way into the main arena of Liberation Square. Suddenly, all attention was turned to them. Jackson, who had by now been ushered to the rostrum for his epoch-making speech, waited as the youth disrupted the inauguration.

Within seconds, a lot happened. Only a keen observer could perceive the events that led to the confusion that followed.

The mobile police team, upon noticing the dissident group, mistook them for supporters of the MCTI. But when it dawned on them that they were indeed intruders, they descended on them with batons and rubber bullets.

The group fought back. Unidentified flying objects were spotted in the air coming from all directions. The rostrum on which Jackson and his loyalists stood erupted in fire as an object exploded, sending people in all directions. More and more explosions were heard within seconds. The mobile police added the straw that broke the camel's back: they fired live bullets and tear gas. There was a great stampede as people ran for safety, all gasping for breath.

At last, the menacing and agile-looking mobile police were left all alone in Liberation Square.

* * *

Dauda Ahmed looked at his watch and saw that it was 9:35 p.m. He went to a public telephone booth and dialed Jackson's hotel room. There was a pause, and the operator connected him to Jackson.

"Hello, Jackson?" Ahmed whispered into the phone.

"Yes, Jackson on the line."

"I am coming over. I wanted to confirm your presence first."

"All right," replied Jackson in a hoarse and shaky voice, "I am expecting you."

The line was dead and Dauda Ahmed picked up his suitcase and the new portfolio he bought that afternoon. It was a beautiful portfolio that cost him a fortune. He bought it especially for the last operation. He opened the portfolio and checked the contents—the bomb was still intact. He checked the connections on the bomb to ensure they were okay, and then he set the timer and closed the portfolio. The bomb would be activated in twenty-five minutes.

He usually wore disguises when he went on missions. He checked his appearance in the standing mirror—he was checking for consistency. After a short while, he nodded to himself in satisfaction. He then picked up his suitcase and the portfolio and surveyed the room once again. There was no trace of Dauda Ahmed. He smiled to himself and closed the door behind him. Once outside, he hailed a taxi and headed to Jackson's hotel room.

At the hotel reception, Dauda Ahmed was attended to promptly because Jackson had informed them he was expecting a guest. Soon, Ahmed got to the elevator and headed to the fifth floor. He checked his wrist watch again—ten minutes remained.

He rapped on the door, and Jackson swung the door open to let his guest in.

"Did you hear what happened today? And you—" Jackson started to say, but Ahmed cut him short.

"I heard everything. One interesting thing is that Ben Sare is scared of you and your movement—otherwise he would not have gone to those lengths. Anyway, like I told you, I will be leaving tonight. I came here to conclude what I started."

"What?" Jackson asked.

"What I mean is, I came to say good-bye," Ahmed replied and brought out a loaded pistol fitted with a silencer. He fired twice at Jackson, and his target fell backward onto the settee. Afterward, there was silence.

Ahmed went over to the door and locked it. He took a closer look at Jackson and smiled. He never missed his target, and this was no exception.

Ahmed fished inside his pockets and brought out a cigarette. He lit it, inhaled deeply, and checked the time—just five minutes to go.

He placed the portfolio on Jackson's lap, took a final look at the room, and left. He locked the door and put the keys inside his pockets. After, he took the elevator to the ground floor and disappeared into the night.

Rather than take a taxi to the military base where his private jet was waiting, he opted to walk. He had barely walked two hundred meters when the sound of an explosion thundered into the night. He looked back toward the hotel and saw smoke escaping from the fifth floor. Only then did he hail a taxi.

Instead of heading straight to the military base, he asked to be taken to the mayor's residence.

Chapter Sixteen

In the early hours of dawn, Ben Sare had unexpected visitors to his country home. He had just gotten out of bed and was saying his morning prayers when a knock sounded at the door. Immediately after, two fierce-looking soldiers in full regalia entered his room.

Ben stared at them with a questioning look in his eyes. All the time he had been under house arrest, his early morning prayers had never been interrupted. He had made it known to all that he could welcome any harassment, but not during his morning prayers. Instinctively, he knew that something was amiss.

"We have been instructed to bring you to the state capitol," they said.

Ben did not argue with the soldiers. He quietly got dressed, took his pipe, and followed them. They drove off in a military jeep to a destination only known to them. Ben's household and the mobile police on guard were taken aback by the strange twist of events. They all knew that something had gone wrong somewhere, but they waited for events to unfold gradually.

*   *   *

There was great confusion throughout Tembeli Kingdom. The dust raised by news of the arrest of the liberator had barely settled when the news of the bombing of Hotel Chocobambam hit the newsstands and air waves. Aerial pictures of the battered left wing of the hostel were plastered across several newspapers. According to the story, fifty people lost their lives in the explosion, including Jackson.

Throughout Tembeli Kingdom, great fear hung in the air. People stayed in their houses and remained glued to their television sets.

Later in the afternoon, news of the death of the mayor of Tembeli Kingdom was confirmed. The mayor was assassinated in his house sometime around midnight.

As investigations into the massacre continued, arrests were made. At the top of the list was the leader of the Tembeli Liberation Movement, Ben Sare. Also on the wanted list was Tamuna, the leader of the youth guerilla movement.

*   *   *

In the swampy rainforest of Tembeli Kingdom, amid the ghostly vegetation that characterized the vastly devastated habitat, Tamuna and Dagogo stuck to one another in a partnership of unflinching solidarity. When news of the death of Jackson filtered through the town (prior to the official announcement by the mass media), Tamuna ran to Dagogo's house, and they took off without telling anybody their destination.

As they sat on some sickly branches of a once-healthy mangrove tree, they could not help reflecting on the state of affairs in their kingdom. "I tell you, Dagogo, I am afraid," Tamuna confessed.

"Afraid of what," Dagogo inquired.

"The future of the land, brother," Tamuna said, "I smell sabotage in these recent spates of massacre. Do you think the bomb blast was a mere accident?"

Dagogo shook his head and replied, "No I don't."

"Then came the mayor's assassination the same night. Ben Sare was arrested, and we are on the wanted list. Obviously, the government would accuse the liberation movement of masterminding the killings, but we know we did not do it. Why *would* we do it?" he queried.

"The truth is, if we wanted to remove Jackson from the scene, we would have done so without leaving a trace," Dagogo said.

"Then who did it?" Tamuna inquired. Dagogo was silent.

"Whoever killed Jackson had a hand in the death of the mayor. I tell you one thing: I suspect foul play on the part of the government and Oilgate. They have a hundred and one reasons to frame Ben Sare and the liberation movement," Tamuna stated.

"I think you have made a very vital point," Dagogo said, "Right now, the fate of Ben Sare and the liberation movement is uncertain, but I think they will prosecute him in their kangaroo tribunal. By and large, I think he has enough evidence to exonerate himself. Remember, his alibi is airtight: Ben Sare was under house arrest when the killings were done."

"That is definitely true: should they try him in court, he will definitely triumph. But if they go to their absurd tribunal, darkness looms ahead," Tamuna said.

"You sound very pessimistic, Tamuna."

"When I said I was afraid, you did not seem to grasp my thoughts. As things are now, only God can save Ben Sare. They have got him where they want him," Tamuna said.

"Ben Sare will get out of this mess. As for us, the bush remains our home," Dagogo replied.

Tamuna stared at Dagogo before exclaiming, "Gogo! Did they arrest Kpandei as well?"

"I don't know yet, but considering the fact that he is the vice president of the liberation movement, he is not likely to escape," Dagogo said.

"They can arrest whoever they want to arrest, but I tell you: victory shall be ours in the end," Tamuna said.

Chapter Seventeen

Day by day, Tembeli Kingdom deteriorated. Not one day passed without activists from the liberation movement being arrested. The total number of arrests had risen to a whopping two hundred and fifty.

Out of the lot, only ten had been arraigned before the military tribunal (the ones charged with the murder of Jackson and the mayor). The rest were being held in military detention camps.

Ben Sare, the liberator; Moses Kpandei, the deputy president of the liberation movement; and fifteen other renowned activists of the liberation movement were the ones arraigned before the military tribunal. The chairman of the tribunal rejected their pleas to nominate lawyers of their choice to defend them. Instead, they were given a pool of military lawyers to choose from.

Human right groups throughout the nation cried foul at the kangaroo dispensation of justice being meted out to the detainees. They called on the international community to impose sanctions on the nation.

Canice Menge, the radical lawyer and human rights activist, went on a solo legal mission to defend the detainees amid the government's refusal to try them in a civil court. He sued the government in the international court of justice for distortion of justice and violation of fundamental human rights. Amnesty international condemned the mode of trial and dubbed it a jungle justice.

Meanwhile, within Tembeli Kingdom, things were really falling apart. Intra-community strife and clashes characterized the day-to-day life of the people. Supporters of the late rival activist, Jackson, clashed openly with loyalists of the liberation movement. The rivalry was such that lives were lost on a daily basis. The mobile police had a field day arresting people and throwing them into detention. They did nothing to check the rival clashes.

The kinsmen of the late mayor blamed the death of their brother on the guerilla movement (allegedly formed by Ben Sare). They vowed to avenge the death of their brother, and they threatened that the land would flow with more blood until the spirit of their dead brother was quieted.

The youth clashed continually as they vied for supremacy. Mischievous ones used the breakdown of law and order to perpetuate all kinds of atrocities on the land, including rape and theft.

As Tamuna reflected on all these things, tears rose from his eyes and ran down his cheeks. He turned to his small receiver radio—his sure link to the outside world—and listened. The melody of African highlife music filled the airwaves. Tamuna knew that it was not news time yet, so he switched off the radio.

He got to his feet and paced around the dilapidated room that was once a classroom of the prestigious Tembeli International School. Everything about the school was now in ruins. Tamuna had relocated to the ruins of his school after a one-week sojourn in the creeks. Dagogo refused to go with Tamuna and went home instead. Tamuna's exploration of TIS as a hiding place had paid off: the once-beautiful and once-busy TIS now looked like a graveyard. Into its serene bosom, Tamuna went for succor.

It had been two days since he left home. With the violence and spate of arrests, he decided it was safer to stay clear of home.

Tamuna sneaked out of his hideout in the evenings to forage for fruits in the school's compound. After what seemed like a quarter of an hour later—when the setting sun had gone beyond the horizon—Tamuna turned to his radio once more and listened. It was already news time.

The revelation from the news was shocking: Ben Sare and sixteen of his kinsmen would find out their fate that evening. At the time of the news report, the trial was still going on.

Chapter Eighteen

The national ruling council, the highest ruling body in the nation, told the world (after a series of meetings) that it had confirmed the death sentence passed on Ben Sare and twelve other Tembelites.

According to the spokesman of the NRC, "The decision to hang Ben Sare was taken unanimously." This kicked off a storm of protests across the globe.

The spokesman said, "The NRC unanimously came to a consensus. We scrutinized the papers and were completely satisfied with the proceedings of the tribunal. This is a case of murder, and those so convicted should die by hanging."

Ironically, the decision confirming the death sentence came on the eve of the commonwealth summit in Auckland. Commonwealth leaders in attendance condemned the death sentence and dubbed it unjust. They called for greater sanctions against the nation.

Canice Menge, the renowned lawyer and human rights activist, led a ten-man team from the Muzanga's human rights community to Auckland, New Zealand to address the commonwealth summit on the human rights situation in the nation.

The team, in their twenty-page letter captioned, "The Time Is Now," urged the commonwealth to demand the immediate and unconditional release of all political detainees in Muzanga, including Ben Sare and his fellow kinsmen.

The boss of Oilgate International, Michael Adams (located in London), sent a letter to the head of state pleading for clemency for Ben Sare and others. Also the managing director, William Smith pleaded for clemency for the Tembelites.

Andrew Carpenter, spokesman for the state department in Washington DC, said the United States deplore the trial. The trial was deemed inadequate in terms of its regard for the rights of the accused. The United States Congress had also written separate letters to the head of state warning that execution of the Tembelites would adversely affect U.S. relations with the nation.

*   *   *

Tamuna waited patiently. *Why hasn't Anita shown up?* he wondered.

The first meeting—the encounter Tamuna had with Anita after the gruesome murder of her father, the mayor of Tembeli kingdom at the ruins of Tembeli International School, remained a mystery to him.

Anita had claimed that she had gotten bored staying at home all day. She said she wanted to go somewhere she could have a quiet moment to herself. Into the decrepit ruins of TIS she went. Her driver had protested the choice, but Anita insisted. She told the driver to come back later in the evening to pick her up.

Anita wandered from one end of the compound to another. She could not help but weep at the degradation the citadel of learning had suffered. When she got tired of wandering, she sat down on a log at the foot of a Gmelina tree. She remembered all the times she had sat at the foot of the tree.

She was momentarily unaware of what was happening in her immediate vicinity, but a touch on her shoulder made her jump. She turned, and surprisingly, she beheld Tamuna. At first, they stared at each other, anger and hate radiating from Anita's eyes. Tamuna broke the embarrassing silence by saying, "It has been my desire to get in touch with you. It was fate that brought you here."

Anita said nothing. She merely stared at Tamuna with eyes as cold as steel.

"I learnt of your father's death. Please accept my sympathy."

"You amaze me, Tamuna. You and your so-called movement killed my father, and here you are asking me to accept your sympathy."

"That is why I needed to see you, to tell you what the true story is. Look, Anita, my movement is not responsible for your father's death. Those who killed your father also killed Jackson. The same people blamed the deaths on the liberation movement in order to frame the liberator.

"Can't you see what they have succeeded in doing? They have set us against each other. They have sown seeds of discord among us so we cannot fight as a group. They killed our illustrious sons and put so many in detention. Now we are so powerless that nobody talks about the bastardization and degradation of our land. We are preoccupied with fighting one another."

Anita's eyes started to soften as she realized what Tamuna was saying. Her eyes no longer radiated hate and anger; rather, one could see in them a longing to mend shattered dreams. She wanted to mend her hurt and not being able to grow up with her beloved father. The dream to finish secondary school successfully (and then proceed to a tertiary institution) was now a thing of the past. The dream of living among her people in an atmosphere devoid of acrimony and rancor had become illusive. She broke down in tears, weeping uncontrollably.

At first, Tamuna did not know whether he should take her into his warm embrace and comfort her. He did not know what her reaction would be. Instead, he said, "Anita, some of our beloved ones are dead and gone, but we who are still alive have no future. Our future is bleak. Those who are dead may have the privilege of resting in eternal peace, but we have no peace. I used to think that it was better to be gone, resting in peace, than to be alive and in this kind of shit."

When Anita started to speak again, she was an entirely different individual. Tamuna found comfort in her endearing tone.

"Tamuna, I believe you when you say you did not kill my father. I was waiting to hear you say it. My father is dead and gone. What hope is there for us that are living?"

"Anita, I must tell you one thing: right now, darkness seems to have fallen over Tembeli. If they hang the liberator and the other twelve, we are wrecked. The only person who can feed the flames of the revolution is Moses Kpandei."

"Who is Moses Kpandei?" Anita asked.

"He is the deputy president of the liberation movement. He and three others were discharged and acquitted by the tribunal for lack of evidence. But they, for sure, are not comfortable with him being let loose. I know, sooner or later, they will go for him."

They chatted on and on until Anita indicated her intention to go home. Tamuna longed to see more of her that evening.

Dusk was settling on the desolate Tembeli International School when, all of a sudden, Tamuna felt a very unusual desire to go home. A great force, unknown to him, seemed to be pulling him home. He stormed into the approaching darkness and took the bush path—the shortest way to school—and walked in silence toward his home.

Chapter Nineteen

The Black Maria zoomed through the dusty road, sending a cloud of dust particles in all directions. When it came to an abrupt halt, fierce-looking soldiers, all clad in black, jumped down and brandished their rifles in a menacing manner. Their masks shielded their faces and made their overall appearance more terrifying.

The mechanical noose was waiting like an anxious predator, waiting to take its victims. A small crowd of sympathizers stood about five hundred meters away in a semicircle.

Dozens of heavily armed soldiers stood guard with their guns, watching the crowd for signs of mischief. Three armored tanks could be spotted on the horizon, all pointing in different directions. But if it weren't for the screeching of the tires of the Black Maria and the thundering sound of army boots, the scene seemed serene.

The steel doors of the Black Maria were thrown wide open. Ben Sare and his fellow convicts were led down with their hands and feet bound in handcuffs. The crowd broke into tears as the convicts made their way toward the noose. Ten meters away from the noose, they were motioned to a halt. The convicts were led to the mechanical noose, and their hands were tied to their sides. They were led to an elevated platform, and the noose was placed on their necks. Next,they were blindfolded and told to stand on the elevated platform to receive their last blessing.

From among the crowd, a priest emerged, clutching his Bible. He moved toward the convicts to administer a last blessing to them. Upon seeing the priest, it suddenly dawned on the convicted activists that their last moments on earth had come. They broke into tears.

Ben Sare remained as solid as a rock, though. He maintained his cool and admonished his compatriots: "Why are you crying? Be strong and dry your tears. You are dying for a good cause, and generations yet unborn will live to remember your noble exploits."

"Yes, sir," they chorused in unison. Even in death, the men remained loyal to Ben Sare. Even in death, they believed in him.

The priest gave the convicted activists their last blessings and stepped aside. The noose operator moved closer to Ben Sare, the first victim. The machine that had been waiting to perform its role was suddenly brought to life.

The operator pressed a combination of levers, and the machine swung up and down before standing still. Suddenly, though, Ben was thrown out of the noose. Evidently, the machine had malfunctioned.

Military engineers and technicians worked on the noose for half an hour. They later confirmed it was set for the job. The men tried again, and again, Ben was ejected. The machine had malfunctioned again.

A loud murmur arose from the crowd, and the fierce-looking soldiers were in awe at the recent development. They tried hanging him five more times, but the outcome was the same. The mechanical noose refused to take its victim.

Military men, engineers, and technicians worked on the noose once more and confirmed it was working. The men decided to leave Ben Sare for the time being, however, and approached one of his compatriots.

They tried again and the noose swung up violently. The victim was caught there wriggling in pain and agony. After a couple of minutes had elapsed—long enough for the victim to be fully dead—they brought the noose down, disengaged the lifeless body, and dragged over another man.

Ben Sare waited helplessly as his compatriots were hanged, one after another. When his turn again came, he said to them, "I want to make one last request before I am hanged. I want to speak with my father."

The men obliged his request, and from among the crowd, Ben Sare's aged father emerged. Ben murmured something to his father, and his father broke down in sobs. The old man was yanked off his son at that point. The men suddenly seemed to be in a hurry to finish their business.

Uncontrolled cries arose from the crowd as the mechanical noose swung into action. This time, the men were successful, and Ben Sare, the liberator, hung from the noose until no life was left in him.

*   *   *

When news of the hanging of the liberator and other activists hit the airwaves, it was received with great shock. Tembelites stormed the streets of the capital city and swarmed like soldier ants defying mobile police and army threats. The demonstrators were clad in black. The scene was reminiscent of a macabre march. Children, young men, young women, and the aged took part in the march.

Moses Kpandei, the deputy president of Tembeli Liberation Movement (the one who was tried alongside the executed activists but was discharged and acquitted) led the peaceful demonstration.

Nationwide and across the globe, the activity was the same: more sanctions were imposed on Muzanga Republic.

Groups calling for sanctions included the Tembeli Liberation Movement, the national human rights community, the national association of journalists, religions organizations and students.

The commonwealth suspended the nation's membership as a result of the execution of the environmental activist. Leading nations, including the United States and Britain, recalled their envoys at the capital city for consultations.

Meanwhile,Moses Kpandei - led demonstrators called for the return of a democratically elected government in Muzanga. The TLM also called for the boycott of Oilgate International, the biggest oil company in Muzanga. A large poster of Ben Sare was attached to the gate of the government house. It was covered with flowers and candles in memory of the fallen hero.

The demonstrators shouted slogans such as, "boycott Oilgate" and "we want democracy." They accused Oilgate of doing to Tembeli Kingdom what it could not do in the West: cashing in on the peoples' ignorance and lack of knowledge about environmental issues. They were waging a devastating war on the environment.

The association of national journalists came up with a six-point communiqué as follows:

- We unequivocally condemn the hanging and dub it a premeditated political execution that will further isolate the nation in the civilized international community.

- We doubt the gruesome killings will stop further agitation by the oil producing communities of Tembeli Kingdom. We believe Oilgate needs to end their economic and environmental plunder and stop intimidating other democratic and human rights campaigners.

- We urge the reinstatement of Decree Twenty, under which the Tembeli Civil Disturbances Tribunal was established.

- We maintain that the executed activists were not subjected to a fair hearing because they were not tried in any of the constitutionally established courts—they were arraigned before a militarily constituted special tribunal whose processes were flawed.

- We urge an end to special tribunals because existing courts have the capacity to adjudicate on all matters up to and including alleged murder.

- We condemn Oilgate for instigating the political execution for fear of decreased oil production.

The nation's human rights community (still in Auckland, New Zealand) for the commonwealth summit welcomed the country's suspension from the organization but regretted that lives were lost because the organization did not take prompt and decisive action.

Chapter Twenty

"He is alive. I tell you that with authority."

"What authority? Agada, you are drunk again."

"Who is drunk? Look don't insult me, Ojimi."

"Agada, just a few bottles of liquor and you are completely off your senses. Ben Sare has been hanged. Everybody knows that except you."

"There you go again. How dare you call me a blockhead."

"You called yourself one, not me. I think it's high time I taught you a lesson," Agada said and scrambled to his feet.

He advanced toward Ojimi with clenched fists. Ojimi struggled to his feet, ready to take on his opponent. Agada threw a punch, missed his target, and fell on top of the table, scattering bottles and glasses in the process. People rushed to the scene from other corners of the bar to quell the conflict.

At that moment, Tamuna strolled into the bar. He neither smoked nor drank, but he went to the bar because it served as a forum for dissemination of information. Every evening, people gathered there to discuss the latest events.

When Agada regained his balance, he attempted to break loose once more, to pounce on Ojimi. He didn't get far, though, because he was held back by a dozen waiting hands.

"Calm down, Agada! What is the matter with you? Tamuna asked.

"Can you imagine this rat calling me a blockhead?" he asked, pointing threateningly at Ojimi.

"You called yourself a blockhead," replied Ojimi.

Agada went on to narrate to Tamuna the circumstances that led to his quarrel with Ojimi. Tamuna laid a hand on Agada's shoulder and comforted him.

"Listen, Agada, you are no blockhead even if he called you one. Likewise, Ojimi is no rat. He is a normal human being, just like any of us."

A crowd had gathered. Tamuna, as young as he was, commanded great respect and admiration. He was seen as a rising star, one of the cornerstones on which the great kingdom of Tembeli would stand in the future. Wherever he stood to talk, people were drawn by the magnetic aura of his speech.

"I see no reason why we must not heal the wounds of the past and forge ahead as members of the same family," he said, "When Agada said that Ben Sare was not dead, some of you may not have understood the wisdom behind his words. Yes, Ben has been hanged. But what he stood for, his dreams of seeing our great kingdom free from all manners of subjugation and exploitation—that still lives on. It lives in the minds of all of us, in the minds of all true patriots of this great kingdom.

We have been set against each other. Agada was ready to slog it out with Ojimi. Our illustrious sons—on whom this great kingdom placed its hopes for salvation—have either been killed or detained. A few, like Kpandei, have left the country because they are on the wanted list. Even yours truly is on the wanted list. In the end, they want to leave us shattered, confused, powerless, and purposeless. But God Almighty will not allow such calamity to befall us, His chosen people. We must bury the hatchet and think about how we can move this great kingdom forward."

A very large crowd had gathered at Liberation Restaurant, and momentarily, the scene was akin to that of a great political event. When Tamuna finished speaking, it was evident that he had calmed all the frayed nerves. It was also clear that he had convinced some Tembelites (those who were ignorant of the different schemes the government used to divide the nation). Some grumbled in low voices, some murmured in comprehension, some shook their heads in awe. Some simply went away without uttering a single syllable, and quite a sizeable number of people stayed behind to have some booze and other local delicacies.

Tamuna walked out into the approaching darkness of dusk. He then headed for home.

*   *   *

Engulfed in the euphoria of being airborne, lost in the awe of being flown above a beautiful island in a jet whose form he could not easily describe—Tamuna had one thing in mind: to make a landing somewhere amid the beautiful floodlit streets of the island.

At last the jet made a safe landing. Tamuna alighted from the jet, accompanied by the crème de la crème of society. He looked around the airfield, and there was great fanfare. Women and children danced in beautiful regalia. Men were clad in all kinds of traditional outfits, and they had hopeful smiles on their faces. They had all come to receive him.

An honor guard was present, and Tamuna walked through the men. In the end, he exchanged pleasantries with lots of dignitaries. The last of the dignitaries made a great impression on Tamuna. He was middle-aged man. He smiled at Tamuna as he approached and extended his hand. Tamuna grabbed the extended hand and murmured his pleasure. Tamuna tried to figure out the man's face, but he could not. He knew he had met the man before, but he could not remember where or when.

A pipe dangled from one end of the man's lips. While smoking, the man heaped praise on Tamuna. He presented Tamuna with a staff, which he then examined. It was a beautiful staff. The handle was made of a material that glittered. At the tip of the staff, there was something like a flame. He could not tell what substance it was made of.

Tamuna raised the staff into the air, and great shouts of jubilation went into the air. When Tamuna brought the staff down, he was alone. He looked around, but there was not a single soul around him. He clutched the staff tightly and walked off.

He raised the staff to the air once more, and something like a motion picture appeared before him on a screen. There, he saw streets as well planned as they were beautiful. The streets shone. Street lights cast different colors of lights that added to the beauty of the environment.

From a distance, Tamuna saw the torch of the Tembeli Kingdom. The gigantic gas-flaring torch was illuminating the environs. Although the torch burnt with in its characteristic manner, no smoke was produced. It was a smokeless, gas-flaring device. Tamuna surveyed the environment for signs of pollution, but there were none.

Tamuna walked down the beautiful streets. He saw a crowd approaching him. He was not afraid because he still held the flaming staff in his hands. When the group approached, he saw that it consisted of teenagers, all carrying placards. They were not engaged in angry protest; their faces radiated happiness. The placards carried many messages. Some expressed thanks to the government for making them beneficiaries of primary, secondary, and tertiary schools' scholarship schemes. Some simply thanked the government for giving them the opportunity to acquire skills such as welding, fitting, carpentry, etc. Tamuna simply waved to the people as they passed.

Behind the first group came another group of men and women. Their ages ranged from early twenties to late thirties. They also carried placards and marched with great excitement toward Tamuna. When they approached him, Tamuna caught a glimpse of the inscriptions on their placards.

The people were grateful to both the government and the oil company operating in the area for being religiously committed to the environment. Some of the inscriptions were expressions of gratitude to the oil company for being committed to operating within their host communities in an environmentally friendly manner. There were too many messages to commit to memory.

Some placards expressed appreciation for the government making the people determiners of their own future. They thanked the government for giving their sons and daughters preferential treatment with regards to employment opportunities in the oil and gas sector of the economy and making some of their daughters ministers and commissioners. Again, the messages on the placards were too many to commit to memory.

Two special groups were the last to participate in the glorious march. The way they marched demonstratively revealed that they were farmers. They had wide, circular raffia hats on their heads, and some had hoes slung over their shoulders. Some carried small fishing nets. They sang and danced. Two men led the group with placards expressing appreciation that the oil companies provided adequate compensation for damages to the fishing nets, fish ponds, crops, trees, and environment as a whole.

Tamuna marveled at the uniqueness of the island that had been entrusted to his care. He was the bearer of the flaming staff. He raised it into the air, and great shouts of jubilation went into the air. The beautiful jet on which he had flown appeared. Tamuna was led to the waiting jet. He got onto the jet and it maneuvered its way through the airfield and disappeared into the sky. Tamuna looked out through the window, and the aerial view of the island made a remarkable impression on his mind.

The jet cruised around the island. After a few hours, the voice of the pilot echoed through the microphone, and he babbled in incoherent syllables. There was distress in his voice. Tamuna tried to figure out what the pilot was saying, but he could not. Suddenly, the jet banked sharply and started diving downward. Tamuna looked out of the window, and a spasm of fear engulfed him. The pilot had lost control of the jet, and they were heading for a crash landing.

Tamuna let out a cry: "Oh God, save us! God, save us! Father, save us! It is our right to exist!"

The jet raced downward toward a cluster of trees in the forest. Tamuna felt a strong force pulling him out of his seat. He was pulled out of his seat, out of the window, and onto what looked like a parachute. And then he hit the ground.

He attempted to get up, and he felt a sharp pain in his ribs. He looked around, and there was darkness. He felt around the immediate vicinity with his fingers. He felt no grass, no trees. He saw no jet.

He had fallen from his bamboo bed and hit the floor. He got up clumsily, opened the door, and went outside. He sat on his father's traditional stool and tried to relax, but it was all in vain. From the direction of his father's hut came the sound of the grandfather clock. It's chimes told him it was midnight. Besides that sound, though, everything was still.

Tamuna looked skyward and beheld the soot-bearing torch of Oilgate's gas flare. What a contrast to what he had seen in his dream. It dawned on him that he was still a peasant boy growing up in an impoverished oil-producing community in Muzanga. He thought about dozens of Tembelites, sons who were currently languishing in detention. He thought about the divisive machinations of the government that had put a knife on the thing that held everyone together. He thought about the acrimony and enmity reigning supreme in Tembeli Kingdom. Tamuna thought about a lot of things.

His childhood dream had been to get as much learning as he could. It had been his dream to be trained as a lawyer so he could wage a legal battle against Oilgate and the government of the Republic. Now, his dream seemed shattered and unrealistic. The citadel of learning—the once-prestigious Tembeli International School—was now a wreck. Everything about the school was in ruins.

Moreover, the school's certificate examinations had long since come and gone while Tembeli International School lay in ruins. He thought about the flaming staff in his dream and the beautiful island that should have been Tembeli.

He sobbed silently at first, but as he thought more about the goose that laid the golden eggs (and how wretched the goose had become), he sobbed more violently.

There was nobody to comfort him. His comfort lay in tomorrow. Tomorrow held the key—the key to the breaking of all the shackles of oppression against Tembeli. Tomorrow would usher in the Tembeli of his dream. Tomorrow, Moses Kpandei would come back from exile to assume the leadership of the Tembeli Liberation Movement and lead the people of Tembeli to Eldorado . . . like the Moses of biblical times.

Tomorrow, the hands that bore the staff—the shinning staff—would no longer be a dream.

Tamuna was still waiting for and thinking about tomorrow when he fell asleep again.